CORNISH WALKS

TOP WALKS IN EAST CORNWALL

LIZ HURLEY

MUDLARK'S PRESS

First Edition, 2019

ISBN: 978-0-9932180-88

All maps in this publication are reproduced from Ordnance Survey 1:25,000 maps, with the permission of The Controller of Her Majesty's Stationery Office, Crown copyright.

Map locations by Google

Coloured illustrations by Aza Adlam

Photography by Liz Hurley

A CIP catalogue record for this book is available from the British Library.

Mudlark's Press

www.lizhurleywrites.com

AN OVERVIEW OF WALK LOCATIONS

CONTENTS

INTRODUCTION

Welcome to Top Walks in Cornwall. This series is designed to show you the very best parts of Cornwall and features a wide range of walks.

These walks have been extensively tested and are widely praised for their ease of use and accuracy. However, we always recommend you carry an OS map with you and a GPS app on your phone is also a useful tool.

Nearly all the walks are circular so you can walk in either direction, although the guide only explains the route one way. If you want a longer walk, just turnaround and retrace your footsteps for a change of scenery. Some of the shorter walks have a neighbouring walk that they can be linked to.

If you do all the walks and their extensions in this book, you will have walked over 60 miles. You will have travelled past Roman forts and Tudor castles, walked the paths of ancient saints, followed streams and rivers down to the sea and beyond. You will have stood in the place of lost estates and hidden wonders and hopefully also spotted some Cornish wildlife as well.

As these are largely countryside / coastal walks, the majority will not be suitable for wheelchairs or buggies.

Each walk is accompanied by notes about various sights along the route. These interesting snippets help bring the walk to life. The guide also recommends other nearby attractions as well as great places to eat and drink locally.

At the back of the book, there are some bonus features, to enhance your walks. Ranging from recipes, recommended reads and interesting articles.

Added Extras

In this day and age, a book can only be enhanced by adding in links to further information. Each walk features links, as well as a photo gallery of sights from the walk. In the print book, I have shortened long web addresses for ease of typing but have left easily typed links as they are. In the e-book all hyperlinks are active.

TIPS AND ADVICE

COUNTRYSIDE CODE

- Respect the people who live and work in the countryside. Respect private property, farmland and all rural environments.

- Do not interfere with livestock, machinery and crops.

- Respect and, where possible, protect all wildlife, plants and trees.

- When walking, use the approved routes and keep as closely as possible to them.

- Take special care when walking on country roads.

- Leave all gates as you find them and do not interfere with or damage any gates, fences, walls or hedges.

- Guard against all risks of fire, especially near forests.

- Always keep children closely supervised while on a walk.

- Do not walk the Ways in large groups and always maintain a low profile.

- Take all litter home - leaving only footprints behind.

- Keep the number of cars used to the minimum and park carefully to avoid blocking farm gateways or narrow roads.

- Minimise impact on fragile vegetation and soft ground.

- Take heed of warning signs – they are there for your protection.

Cattle
- If you find yourself in a field of suddenly wary cattle, move away as carefully and quietly as possible, and if you feel threatened by cattle then let go of your dog's lead and let it run free rather than try to protect it and endanger yourself. The dog will outrun the cows, and it will also outrun you.

- Those without canine companions should follow similar advice: move away calmly, do not panic and make no sudden noises. Chances are the cows will leave you alone once they establish that you pose no threat.

- If you walk through a field of cows and there happen to be calves, be vigilant, as mothers can be more protective. If crossing a field with cattle in, you don't need to stick to the footpath if you wish to avoid them. By all means, skirt around the edge of the field.

- Remain quiet. Cows are curious, if they hear a lot of noise they will come over and investigate.

Walking with dogs
- The Coast Path is unfenced, and the cliffs can have sheer drops. Every year dogs die, running off the edge, so it is always safest to keep your dog on a lead.

- Please pick up after your dogs and always take the bag home if you can't find a bin.

- All the walks in this book are suitable for dogs on leads.

GUIDE TO THE LEGEND

Before heading off for a walk read the description first. You may discover issues with it. Cows, tides, number of stiles, mud etc. Then have a look at a map, not just the little one provided with the walk, to get a proper feel for the direction of the walk.

ADDITIONAL INFORMATION: Some walks may be hampered by the tide or weather, or may be improved by a few specific suggestions. Detail will be given here.

OPTIONAL WALK: Occasionally, a walk will have a smaller sidewalk nearby. This won't be described in length but mentioned as a suggestion.

LENGTH: This has been calculated using a range of GPS tracking devices but ultimately we have used the Ordnance Survey route tracker. This will generally differ from a pedometer.

EFFORT: Easy to Challenging. These descriptions are only in relation to each other in this book. Every walk has at least one hill in it; not everyone finds hills easy. Challenging, this is for the hardest walks in the book, it will be based on effort and duration. However, nothing in here is particularly tortuous.

TERRAIN: If it's been raining a lot, please assume that footpaths will be muddy. Coastal paths tend to be a bit better, near villages they tend to be a bit worse. During the end of summer, vegetation may obscure the path.

FOOTWEAR: This is a suggestion for terrain rather than weather. After rain or winter, trainers may not provide enough protection. It is always down to a personal preference as to what to walk in.

LIVESTOCK: It is possible that you won't encounter any livestock on a walk that mentions them. Please read the Countryside Code section, on how to avoid them if you do.

PARKING: Postcode for sat nav given, when a specific car park is mentioned be aware, Cornwall is not always kind to sat navs, have a road map to hand and check you know where you are heading before you set off.

WCs: Due to council cuts, lots of loos are now closed or run by local parishes with seasonal opening hours. If they are an essential part of your walk, check online first. Lots are now coin operated.

CAFÉ / PUB: Local recommendations. Always check ahead, some will have seasonal opening hours.

OS MAP: This will be the largest scale available for the area.

NEARBY ATTRACTIONS: These are sites worth visiting within a short drive of the walk's location. Some will be seasonal and may have an admission charge.

DIRECTIONS: If I say, "going up the road" up or down means there is a slope. If I refer to North or SW, you will need a compass. Most smartphones have built-in compasses. It won't be essential as other directions will be given, but it will be an aide. Especially in woodland where there are few other clues.

FINALLY

Things change: Trees fall down, posts get broken, signs become obscured, footpaths can be closed for repair. Do not be alarmed if you can't see a marker.

1
....

BUDE VIA COAST AND CANAL

A breath-taking walk across the cliffs leaving Bude behind and then cutting inland across fields. Finishing with a gentle stroll back along the Bude Canal. A great opportunity for bird spotting.

OPTIONAL WALK: The towpath from Bude to Helebridge is flat and tarmacked all the way. This would be perfect for wheelchairs and buggies. There and back it's a distance of 3 miles. Bikes are not permitted.

LENGTH: 6 miles
EFFORT: Moderate
TERRAIN: Coast Path, fields, tow path
FOOTWEAR: Trainers will be fine in dry weather
LIVESTOCK: Some potential for sheep
PARKING: Tourist Information car park, Bude
WCs: Bude
CAFÉ / PUB: Bude – Various
OS MAP: 111

NEARBY ATTRACTIONS: Bude Sea Pool, an absolute must. Devon!

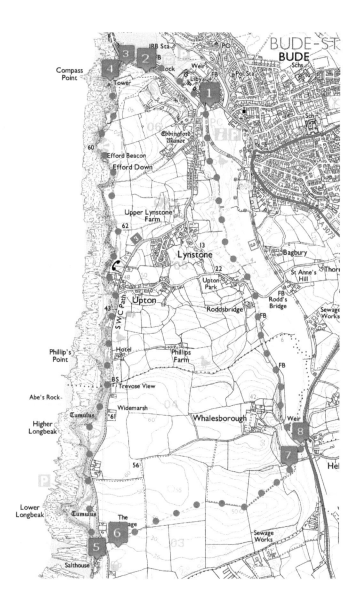

Elevation Profile

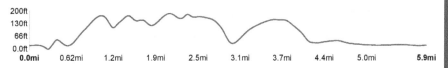

200ft									
130ft									
66ft									
0.0ft									
0.0mi	0.62mi	1.2mi	1.9mi	2.5mi	3.1mi	3.7mi	4.4mi	5.0mi	5.9mi

STORM TOWER

DIRECTIONS:

1. From the Tourist Information car park cross the road towards the Post Office. Walk just past it and then turn right onto the canal tow path. Follow the canal down towards the sea and just before you reach the sea cross over the canal via the sluice gates.

Storm Tower:
This pretty octagonal tower was based, loosely, on the Temple of the Winds in Athens. It was built to provide shelter for the coastguards and was designed by George Wightwick for Sir Thomas Acland. There were

2. Now turn right and walk a short distance until you reach a flight of steps by East Cottage. Head up the steps and then turn right. Walk past the large ornamental lamp post and head up the next small flight of steps.

3. Turn right and head out towards the water. You are now on the Coast Path and will stay on this for the next 2 miles. There is an option to walk out onto the promontory which gives some lovely views over to the *sea pool*. Watch out for waves at high tide.

4. Continue along the Coast Path and head up to the octagonal folly, known as the *Storm Tower*. Having had a quick explore continue on the path. When you get to a bench near a stone wall, the path continues through a kissing-gate on your left. The cliffs along this stretch are high and crumbly. Stay away from the edge and pay attention to any diversions. Keep dogs and children on a lead.

some that dismissed this as simply a folly, but it seems that the landowner clearly believed that something functional could also be ornamental. As you walk around it you can see the names of the Winds carved at the top.

i **Bude Canal:**
This is a broad canal that was built to deliver fertilisers and lime to the local farms. The minerals in the local sand greatly improved the poor agricultural land and the canal was built to carry the sand inland. Today only the first short section of the canal remains, running from the sea lock gates up to the first of the inclined planes. Rather than using locks to navigate the rising topography, the engineers built a series of inclined planes that, through the use of chains and

BUDE CANAL

5.   Having walked the 2 miles from Bude the path comes down into Widemouth Bay. You will see the long sandy beach ahead of you, this is a popular surfing spot. Just as you reach the beach the path has to snake around a set of white cottages. Turn left and walk along their driveway up to the main road. Cross directly over the road and into a field. The footpath is signed 'Helebridge 1 mile'.

6.   The path now crosses through a series of fields. In this first field, turn left and follow the hedge up to its top left corner. Cross the track and head directly into the field ahead, ignoring those to the left and right. The path heads through the middle of the field on a left-hand angle but is clear to see on the ground.

waterwheels, hauled the specially adapted tub boats up onto the next level of the canal.

Sea Pool:
You can't visit Cornwall and not swim in one of the sea water swimming pools and Bude has one of the largest and most easily accessible. Sea pools were built to offer the locals the ability to swim in the curative properties of sea water without any of the risks of waves and rip tides. Bude's was built in the 1930s and has been in use ever since. It's certainly a wonderful experience.

BUDE SEA POOL

Walking through into the next field, stick to the track on the right-hand side. Continue along this track into the next field heading downhill towards a road. At the bottom, pass through a kissing-gate and into a paddock, walk forward and then downhill. You will come out at a kissing-gate in the left-hand corner of the paddock.

7.   You should now be on the drive for Whalesborough Holiday Park. Turn right and when you get to the private car park turn into it and walk through towards the river and *Bude Canal*. At the footpath turn left following the towpath sign to Bude.

8.   Finally walk along the towpath for 1½ miles. At one point the towpath will cross over to the right-hand side via a small bridge. It will finish at the original Tourist Information car park.

DODGING THE WAVES

LINKS:

Bude Canal
http://www.bude-canal.co.uk/Bude%20Canal%20History.htm
Bude Sea Pool
https://www.budeseapool.org/

PHOTO ALBUM:

https://flic.kr/s/aHsmbYZLDT

2

ANCIENT PATHS
AROUND TINTAGEL

A stunning walk taking in the landscape of myths and legends, passing through fields and a rocky valley leading down to the sea, then along the dramatic north coast until you come across the ancient castle of Tintagel and suggested site for the birthplace of the legendary King Arthur.

OPTIONAL WALK: The *St Nectan's Glen* walk can be easily included in this walk. It features Cornwall's most atmospheric waterfall. There is an entry charge and a lot of steps.

LENGTH: 7 miles (9 if including St Nectan's extension)
EFFORT: Strenuous
TERRAIN: Coast Path, fields, lanes
FOOTWEAR: Walking boots or heavy footwear recommended
LIVESTOCK: Some potential for sheep
PARKING: Tintagel
WCs: Tintagel
CAFÉ / PUB: Napoleon Inn at Boscastle
OS MAP: 111

NEARBY ATTRACTIONS: Tintagel Castle, English Heritage. Museum of Witchcraft and Magic, Boscastle

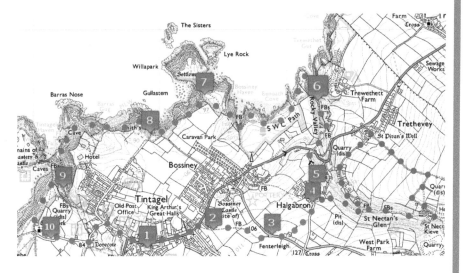

Elevation Profile

TINTAGEL PUFFINS

DIRECTIONS:

1. From the Tourist Information Centre walk out of the car park and turn right. Walk along the road heading away from the village centre. As you pass the turning for Trenale on your right, keep an eye out for a footpath sign also on the right. Take this path into a field by climbing over the first in a series of slate coffer stiles. Walk in the direction of a large granite post and about ten metres before it, head over another stile on your left.

2. The path now cuts across three large fields. It should be apparent but there is also a red marker at each stile to help you work out which direction to walk in. The fields are

Tintagel Castle:
Oh, Tintagel. What hasn't been written about the mythical birthplace of King Arthur, Britains' most legendary figure? Looking at the impregnable fortress perched above the sea one can understand how all the stories sprang up. It positively embraces them, with the booming sea caves below, the sudden rolling mists, the epic storms. It's hard to imagine a site more deserving of a good tale. Follow the links below to learn more.

likely to have sheep in them and can be very muddy after heavy rain. The stiles may be very difficult for very large dogs.

3.　As you leave the final field turn right and walk along the road. Just after you pass the garage for Fenterleigh House keep an eye out for a footpath sign on the left. This takes you through a five-bar gate and into a private driveway, however it is a right of way running along the drive and courtyard. The path then continues over a stile and into a field. Looking across the field you want to head towards the left-hand gate. Just to the right of that gate, there are some stepping stones through the hedge, climb over these and onto the lane. Now walk left, down the lane until you reach a footpath on your right, by a five-bar gate. Step 4 offers a fascinating detour to visit St Nectan's Glen, otherwise go to Step 5.

4.　If you want to visit St Nectan's Glen with the waterfalls, climb the stile beside the gate, and head across the middle of the field, walking towards the line of trees. Go through the rusted, ornate metal gate and walk down through the trees until you get to a bridge which you should cross over. Now follow the instructions in Walk 3 *St Nectan's Glen*. You will be joining the walk at Step 3 and then following Steps 4, 1 & 2. It is a full loop so you will be coming back to this point and then return up to the lane at the start of this option.

SIGHTS ON THE ST NECTAN'S WALK

5.   Having completed, or ignored the loop, continue heading downhill until the lane joins a main road. Cross straight over and follow the footpath sign down towards the Coast Path via the *Rocky Valley*. This footpath is well laid out but will be wet and slippery after heavy rain. See if you can find the labyrinth markings as you pass through the ruined buildings of Trevillett Mill and then cross the stream again. This stream is the same one that flows through St Nectan's Glen.

6.   Continue walking with the stream on your right. As you get to the mouth of the valley you will join the Coast Path. Turn left. After a short distance there is an

i Rocky Valley:
Rocky Valley is a gorge cut by a stream that rises up in Venn Down and then plunges down through St Nectan's Glen and onto the sea, creating a dramatic natural feature. Halfway down the path, you will pass through the ruined buildings of Trevillett Mill. Have a look to your right and explore the natural slate walls. Carved into

ROCKY VALLEY

CARVED LABYRINTHS

option to walk forward and explore the stream as it rushes towards the sea. This is a lovely little gorge and worth exploring but dangerous in rough weather as the waves are hidden until the last corner.

7. Now on the Coast Path walk uphill with the sea on your right. The next few miles will be undulating with glorious views. It can be hard work but there are plenty of places to rest. At one point you will head into a section named *Willapark*. During this section the path appears to continue straight on, but you need to turn left just after a bench by a stone wall. If you continue forward the path heads out onto a dramatic headland, known as the

the rock are two labyrinths. Nothing is known about them and whilst they were originally thought to be Bronze Age they are more common in style with mediaeval Christian labyrinths.

SEA MIST ROLLING IN

Willapark Headland. It is worth exploring but otherwise turn left and continue along the Coast Path.

8.   Further along, there is a very obvious split in the path, take the right-hand fork for the Coast Path, the left-hand path takes you back into Tintagel village. Continue along this path until you arrive at Glebe Cliff, take the footpath to the right, head downhill and then when the path splits again, take the left-hand path. You will come to the base of the cliffs that *Tintagel Castle* sits upon. As you look down at the beach you may be able to see Merlin's Cave, depending on the tide.

9.   The path now leads into a Visitors Centre and café. To pick the path up again, walk past the loos and the Coast Path continues up on the right-hand side.

ⓘ Willapark:
Willapark is Cornish for 'enclosure with view' and was once the site of an Iron Age hillfort. This headland offers glorious views up and down the coast line. In summer, if you are lucky, you may also spot visiting Puffins as well as Razorbills and Guillemots. There is also a second named Willapark, further up the coast near Boscastle which was also home to an Iron Age settlement.

Zigzagging upwards the footpath runs alongside one of the castle's outbuildings and upper entrance. As you climb to the top of the cliffs, look behind and you will get a real sense of the drama of Tintagel Castle. Continue along the well-made footpath until you get to the path that heads toward St Materiana's Church. There is a Roman milestone here, standing in the south transept.

10. Leave the Churchyard on the road-side and follow the lane left, heading back into the village. This is a narrow lane without a footpath so watch out for traffic. When the lane joins the main road, turn right. Walk along this road, crossing the small roundabout and continue until you reach the Tourist Information Centre and the end of your walk.

FRIENDLY FACES

LINKS:

Tintagel

https://www.english-heritage.org.uk/visit/places/tintagel-castle/

King Arthur and Cornwall

http://www.king-arthur.co.uk/home/tintagel

PHOTO ALBUM:

https://flic.kr/s/aHskQTRMTg

3

ST NECTAN'S GLEN

There is a charge to visit the waterfall itself. However, it is a beautiful site. The rest of the walk heads through a wooded valley and explores a Roman marker, a holy well and an ancient chapel.

OPTIONAL WALK: This walk can be added to the *Tintagel* walk.

LENGTH: 2 miles
EFFORT: Moderate – lots of steps
TERRAIN: Woodland trails
FOOTWEAR: Trainers are fine, but it can be very wet in parts. St Nectan's Glen provides wellies
LIVESTOCK: None
PARKING: St Nectan's Glen car park on the main road
WCs: St Nectan's Glen
CAFÉ / PUB: St Nectan's Glen
OS MAP: 111

NEARBY ATTRACTIONS: Tintagel Castle, English Heritage. Museum of Witchcraft and Magic, Boscastle

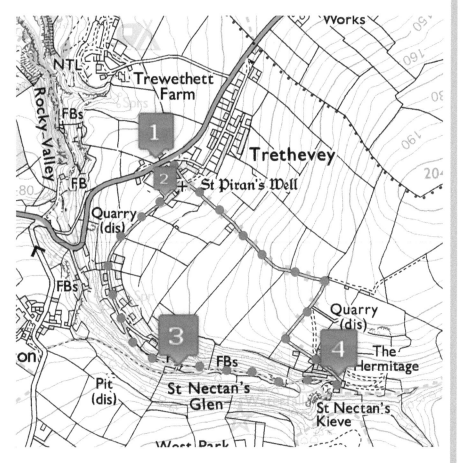

Elevation Profile

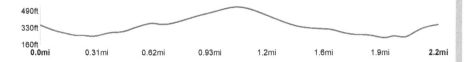

490ft
330ft
160ft
0.0mi   0.31mi   0.62mi   0.93mi   1.2mi   1.6mi   1.9mi   2.2mi

21

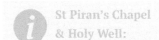
CLOUTIE TREE

DIRECTIONS:

1. From the car park cross the road and follow the private lane up to the hamlet of Trethevy and *St Piran's Holy Well*.

2. In front of *St Piran's Chapel* turn right and head along the tarmacked lane. As you pass between the cottages keep an eye out on your right for the *Roman milestone*. Continue along the lane until it ends at two private drives and a pathway. Take the pathway heading downhill into the wooded valley and walk along the valley floor.

3. Walk past the footbridge that crosses the river, this is where you will join

St Piran's Chapel & Holy Well:

The chapel was first mentioned in 1457 but was converted into an agricultural building after the reformation. In 1941 the building was returned to the Church of England. The first mass was celebrated in 1944 and the previous owner promptly died the next day. Across the lane is a small holy well with an odd stone cap that might be a re-purposed font and is again dedicated to St Piran. Given the proximity to St

STACKED STONES

if you are coming in from the Tintagel walk. Continue walking upstream until you get to St Nectan's Visitor Centre. There is a nice café and some loos here. Entrance to the waterfall is charged and only available during the daytime. The Centre will provide wellies. You will see that the trees in the area are covered in strips of cloths, these are known as *clouties* and have a spiritual significance.

Nectan's Glen and hermitage, the naming of these two sites after St Piran is unusual, especially as St Piran is better associated with West Cornwall.

i **Roman Milestone:**
On the lane near the Chapel is a Roman milestone inscribed C DOMI N GALLO ET VOLUS which translates as 'For the Emperor

ST NECTAN'S KIEVE

4. Having explored the waterfall, continue around on your loop. Take the lane by the outside loos and start walking uphill along the unmade lane. This will take you all the way back to the hamlet of Trethevy, where you can now return to your car.

CLOUTIE OFFERINGS

Caesars our lords Gallus and Volusian'. Dating to the third century, circa 251 - 253, it is only one of five in Cornwall. First re-discovered in 1919 it was being used as a nearby gate post. There is another Roman milestone in the churchyard of St Matariana in Tintagel.

i **Clouties:**
Largely associated with Celtic water spirits, a cloutie or clootie is a scrap of cloth that is tied to a tree to ask for healing or blessing. With its Celtic past and large number of wells, springs and waterfalls, Cornwall has lots of places that are festooned with clouties. St Nectan's Glen is a particularly good example of an age-old belief system still flourishing.

LINKS:

St Piran's Chapel and Holy Well
https://www.britainexpress.com/counties/cornwall/churches/trethevy.htm
St Nectan's Glen
https://www.st-nectansglen.co.uk/

PHOTO ALBUM:

https://flic.kr/s/aHskQTRMTg

4
....

THE RUMPS AT POLZEATH

An easy circular cliff walk. Dramatic views along the north coast and a great opportunity to spot sea birds and wildflowers. There's also the chance to walk onto Cornwall's most stunning example of an Iron Age hillfort.

LENGTH: 3 miles
EFFORT: Easy to moderate
TERRAIN: Coast Path
FOOTWEAR: Trainers will be fine in dry weather
LIVESTOCK: Some possibility for sheep and Highland cattle
PARKING: Lead Mines National Trust car park. PL27 6QY
WCs: Polzeath (1 mile)
CAFÉ / PUB: Polzeath (1 mile)
OS MAP: 106

NEARBY ATTRACTIONS: St Enodoc Church, resting place of John Betjeman. Pencarrow House

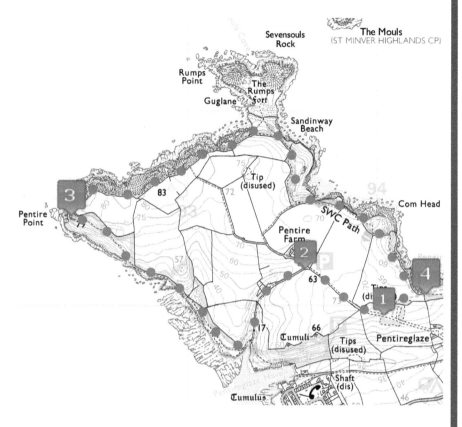

Elevation Profile

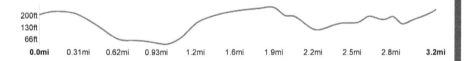

200ft										
130ft										
66ft										
0.0mi	0.31mi	0.62mi	0.93mi	1.2mi	1.6mi	1.9mi	2.2mi	2.5mi	2.8mi	**3.2mi**

THE RUMPS

DIRECTIONS:

1. From the car park head onto the private road and turn right, walking towards the sea. At the end of the road go through the small gate beside the larger farm gate, the path is very clearly laid out. As you get to the farm buildings, take the footpath on your left which is well signposted.

2. You are heading down to Pentireglaze Haven along a pretty, high-banked path. As you come down to the beach the path splits left and right, take the right-hand fork. From here on, dogs should be on leads as there are sheer drops along the way. You are now on the Coast Path.

The Rumps:
The Rumps are a headland on which an Iron Age hillfort, also known as a cliff castle, once stood. No buildings remain but the original ramparts are still very clear and as you walk onto the headland you will pass through the neck of three distinct lines of defence. Very little is known about who built the hillfort or what it was used for but there is evidence of some form of occupation up until the first century AD.

Follow for the next ¾ of a mile until you arrive at a large granite outcrop known as Pentire Point.

3.   From here continue along the Coast Path, soon you will see *The Rumps* ahead of you, there are two clear paths on your left if you want to explore the Iron Age hillfort. Highly recommended, if only for the views. Look up the coast to your right and see if you can spot Tintagel Castle. From here return to the Coast Path and continue.

i **Flora & Fauna:** During spring and summer, this section of coastline is awash with wildflowers. The fields turn pink, blue and yellow as swathes of flowers come into bloom, whilst in later summer the heather and ferns dominate. Out to sea, you might spot pods of dolphins or the odd smaller whale and in early summer you would be in a good position to see the massive basking sharks. On the beaches below, seals often congregate as

SEA PINKS

COASTAL PATH

4.   As you walk ignore any footpath sign returning you to Pentire Farm. When you get to a small gate on the Coast Path and another on your right, turn right into the field. This will be about a mile from The Rumps. Once in the field turn right and walk through the field toward the small rise and scrubland, the path is clear in the grass. Lead Mines car park is just beyond this scrub section.

they are unlikely to be disturbed. Overhead this is a popular spot for peregrine falcons as well as kestrels and ravens. The Rumps and Pentire Point provide some of the best seabird watching in Cornwall; Gannet, Fulmar, Cormorant, Shags, Kittiwake, Razorbill, Guillemot can be seen at any time of the year. Also, keep your eye open for the Chough and even, occasionally, Puffins.

LINKS:

Cornwall – Area of Outstanding Natural Beauty
http://www.cornwall-aonb.gov.uk/pentirepointtowidemouth
The Rumps
http://www.historic-cornwall.org.uk/a2m/iron_age/cliff_castle/the_rumps/the_rumps.htm
Cornish Wildlife
http://www.wildlifeinsight.com/seawatching-in-cornwall/the-rumps-and-pentire-point-guide-to-watching-dolphins-seals-basking-sharks-and-seabirds/

PHOTO ALBUM:

https://flic.kr/s/aHsmDB9VPL

5

PADSTOW TO STEPPER POINT

A wonderful walk across fields, cliffs and beaches. Despite the length, this is an easy walk with great views in all directions. One for lovers of big skies and distant horizons.

LENGTH: 7 miles
EFFORT: Easy
TERRAIN: Coast Path, fields, paths, small road
FOOTWEAR: Trainers will be fine in dry weather
LIVESTOCK: Cattle and sheep likely
PARKING: Padstow Link Road car park. PL28 8AX
WCs: Padstow. Rest A While Tea Gardens (seasonal)
CAFÉ / PUB: Padstow. Rest A While Tea Gardens (seasonal)
OS MAP: 106

NEARBY ATTRACTIONS: Prideaux Place. National Lobster Hatchery. Padstow Sea Life Safari. Cornish Birds of Prey Centre

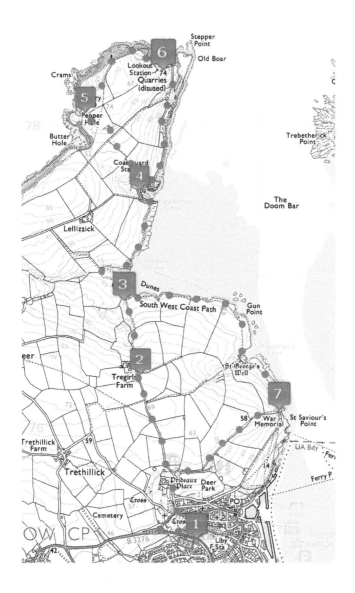

Elevation Profile

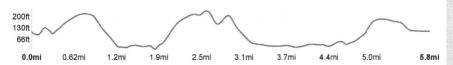

200ft									
130ft									
66ft									
0.0mi	0.62mi	1.2mi	1.9mi	2.5mi	3.1mi	3.7mi	4.4mi	5.0mi	5.8mi

LOOKING OUT TO SEA

DIRECTIONS:

1. From the Link Road car park, head out towards the road and then turn right so you are walking uphill, then take the first road on your right. As you approach the entrance for Prideaux Place, turn right, and then walk along Tregirls Lane with the Prideaux walls on your left. Continue along this road for half a mile. It is a dead end and only serves the farm at the far end, so traffic is minimal but be aware.

2. As you approach Tregirls Farm the footpath is clearly labelled continuing first to the right-hand side of the buildings and then running down the side of

The Doom Bar:
As you look out over Padstow Bay when the tide is out you can't fail to notice the sand bars that spread across the mouth of the bay. The largest and worst of these is The Doom Bar, which is particularly difficult because it has been known to move dramatically after storms. The sand bars are invisible at high tide and when a sailing vessel would head into the bay the cliffs would block the wind and the ships would suddenly be prone to

the fields. To your right are glorious views over Padstow Bay and *The Doom Bar*. Ahead in the distance is a large tower that you are heading to. Follow the path downhill until you reach a T-junction.

3. Turn left following the signs for the Coast Path, you will cross over a little causeway and the path turns inland for a bit as it navigates a lush creek. As you cross another causeway turn right and immediately ahead of you are a couple of steps (often obscured by bushes) up onto the Coast Path. Stay on this path until you reach the Coastguard cottages at Hawker's Cove.

OUT ONTO THE COAST PATH

THE DOOM BAR HIDING BELOW THE WATER

4.   Follow the path through the hamlet and just before the kissing gate take the left-hand footpath. There are also signs to Rest A While Tea Gardens. Head up the path, over a stile and into a field. Walk uphill, with the hedge on your right, through another field and then leave via a stile. Now walk forwards until you re-join the Coast Path and then turn right. The cliffs are very high here and there may also be cattle.

5.   Follow the Coast Path up to the large tower. This is a Daymark tower used for navigational purposes and the headland you are on is known as Stepper Point. From the Daymark head on towards the Coastguard Lookout Station.

6.   From the Lookout Station take the Coast Path all the way back to Padstow following the post markers all the way. You will have walked sections of it on the way here. When you get to the creek section from Step 3 you can turn left and walk through the dunes for a change of scene. The path through the dunes is very clear and re-joins the Coast Path proper further along. Eventually, the path reaches the edge of Padstow where there are large metal gates and a large Celtic cross. From Stepper Point to the gates is about 2 miles.

drifting onto the sand bars. Over the centuries there have been countless shipwrecks.

Legend has it that The Doom Bar came into existence when a young man shot a girl that spurned him. However, he hadn't realised she was a mermaid, and in her fury, she threw a great bank of sand across the bay. The lessons to be learnt here are don't shoot people and don't annoy mermaids.

Padstow:
Whilst Padstow originally grew as a fishing village, and it does still have a fishing industry, it is now better known as a tourist attraction and food destination due to Rick Stein's fish restaurant. From opening this in 1975 his reputation and restaurants grew; he published books and became a well-known TV personality. This connection has earnt Padstow the nickname of PadStein. Since then the town and surrounding coast have become known for offering the best dining in Cornwall and gradually this effect has rippled out all over Cornwall. I recommend you try the fish dish.

STEPPER DAYMARK

7.   To return to the car park and Prideaux Place, turn right into a field just before the gates and follow the clear footpath. The views are stunning. At the end of the footpath, just before the lane there is a spring on the right known as Fenton Leno. Turn left onto the lane and you should recognise that you are once more back on Tregirls Lane where you can retrace your steps to the car park. Alternatively, at the gates, continue along the path and head into Padstow. It's an easy route from Padstow back up to the Link Road car park.

LINKS:

Myths and Legends of The Doom Bar

https://ztevetevans.wordpress.com/2016/01/13/the-legend-of-the-doom-bar-of-padstow/

Ghosts of Padstow

https://www.cornwalls.co.uk/myths-legends/padstow.htm#

PHOTO ALBUM:

https://flic.kr/s/aHsmDmvaS6

6

BROWN WILLY AND TWO MORE TORS

Bag three tors, look down over all of Cornwall as you stand on the highest point and enjoy giggling over silly names. The tors are wonderful geological features so don't forget your camera: the wildlife might even pose for a photo.

ADDITIONAL INFORMATION: The weather can change very quickly on the moors. Do not bother with this walk in low visibility. It relies on good visibility as there are no man-made footpaths or regular way posts.

LENGTH: 5½ miles
EFFORT: Moderate
TERRAIN: Moorland
FOOTWEAR: Walking boots or heavy footwear recommended
LIVESTOCK: Cattle, sheep, horses all likely. They will all avoid you
PARKING: Rough Tor car park. PL32 9QG
WCs: Closest Camelford (2 miles)
CAFÉ / PUB: Closest Camelford (2 miles)
OS MAP: 109

NEARBY ATTRACTIONS: Tintagel. Launceston Castle. Jamaica Inn

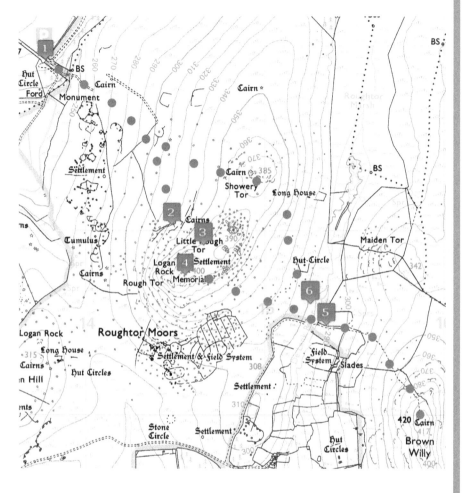

Elevation Profile

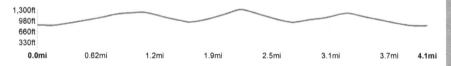

1,300ft							
980ft							
660ft							
330ft							
0.0mi	0.62mi	1.2mi	1.9mi	2.5mi	3.1mi	3.7mi	**4.1mi**

ON TOP OF THE WORLD

DIRECTIONS:

1. From the car park walk down through the gate and cross over the stream. Ahead of you are three *tors*. To your left, standing clearly on its own is Showery Tor, to the far right is Rough Tor and on Rough Tor's left is Little Rough Tor. Walk towards them heading on a path that cuts between Showery Tor and Rough Tor, this is the most gentle ascent. Incidentally, Rough Tor is pronounced Row, to rhyme with Cow. Not Row to rhyme with No or rough to rhyme with gruff.

2. As you get to the foothills of the tors, turn right and start heading towards Rough Tor. There is no one clear path. As you head towards Rough Tor see if you

Cornish Tors:
"A tor is a large, free-standing rock outcrop that rises abruptly from the surrounding smooth and gentle slopes of a rounded hill summit or ridge crest. Tors are landforms created by the erosion and weathering of rock; most commonly granites, but also schists, dacites, dolerites, coarse sandstones and others. Tors are mostly less than 5 metres (16 ft.) high. Each outcrop can comprise several tiers or pillows, which may become separated stacks: rocking pillows are called logan stones. These stacks are vulnerable to frost

ROUGH TOR MEMORIAL

can spot St Michael's Holy Well. It sits on a spring and is a small dressed granite structure. However, given the number of granite boulders around it is hard to spot. There is a stream running down from it so if you find a stream try to follow it up. However, there are lots of little streams.

action and often collapse leaving trails of blocks down the slopes called clitter or clatter. Weathering has also given rise to circular "rock basins" formed by the accumulation of water and repeated freezing and thawing." (Source: Wiki)

3.   Continue up onto Rough Tor, the stone features up here are an incredible sight. With your back to the car park look straight ahead from Rough Tor and you can see *Brown Willy*, this is the highest point in Cornwall.

4.   Make your way off Rough Tor, heading towards Brown Willy and walk down across the moor. Have a look at the map as well, to ensure you are pointing in the right direction. When you get to a field wall, keep it on your right and walk until you cross a stream. On the other side are a gate and stile.

Brown Willy:
The top of Brown Willy is 1,378 feet above sea level and is the tallest point in Cornwall. It's uncertain how it achieved its name but there are a few sources that suggest it comes from the Cornish *Bronn Ewhella* - "Highest Hill". There was a brief campaign in 2012 to change its name back to the Cornish one but it turned out that everyone preferred the giggle factor.

ROUGH TOR

5.   Having crossed the stile, there is a fairly clear path up to the top of Brown Willy. Once at the top, enjoy the views and the fact that you are the highest person in Cornwall. If you look back the way you came you will see Rough Tor to your left and Showery Tor clearly on the right. Now make your way back down to the stile, gate and stream.

6.   Cross the stream once more and now head towards Showery Tor. This is the distinctive tor to your right, the path towards it is fairly obvious, and you will pass an old stone walled enclosure. Having had a rest at the summit of Showery Tor, you can now head back to the car park which is ahead of you.

MOORLAND PONIES

LINKS:

Bodmin Moor

http://www.cornwall-aonb.gov.uk/bodminmoor

PHOTO ALBUM:

https://flic.kr/s/aHsmxNRjfs

7

SIBLYBACK, CHEESEWRING AND THE HURLERS

*A wonderful walk across Bodmin Moor and its tors.
Encompassing wild swimming lakes, ancient stone circles, tin
mins and with wildlife all around. Returning via a small road
section and then across fields and pretty streams.*

ADDITIONAL INFORMATION: The weather can change
very quickly on the moors. Do not bother with this walk
in low visibility. It relies on good visibility as there are no
man-made footpaths or regular way posts.

LENGTH: 7 miles
EFFORT: Moderate
TERRAIN: Mostly moorland, one small stretch of road
FOOTWEAR: Walking boots or heavy footwear recommended
LIVESTOCK: Cattle, sheep, horses all likely. They will all
avoid you
PARKING: Siblyback Visitor Centre car park. PL14 6ER
WCs: Siblyback. Minions
CAFÉ / PUB: Siblyback. Minions
OS MAP: 109

NEARBY ATTRACTIONS: Golitha Falls. Jamaica Inn.
Carnglaze Caverns. Trethevy Quoit

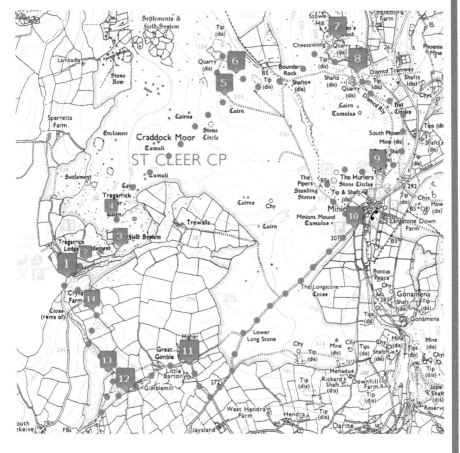

Elevation Profile

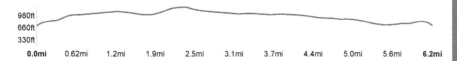

980ft										
660ft										
330ft										

0.0mi 0.62mi 1.2mi 1.9mi 2.5mi 3.1mi 3.7mi 4.4mi 5.0mi 5.6mi **6.2mi**

THE CHEESEWRING

DIRECTIONS:

1. As you approach Siblyback, park in the first overflow car park. Walk in the direction of the lake facilities and immediately take the right-hand lane, heading towards the red post box. Just by the post box, take the footpath on the left.

2. Walk up the path between two stone walls and at the top go through the gate. You are now in an open bit of scrubland. Turn right and head up to a group of trees on the horizon, walking in the direction of a telegraph pole. Walk through the small gate.

Cornish Tors:
"A tor is a large, free-standing rock outcrop that rises abruptly from the surrounding smooth and gentle slopes of a rounded hill summit or ridge crest. Tors are landforms created by the erosion and weathering of rock; most commonly granites, but also schists, dacites, dolerites, coarse sandstones and others. Tors are mostly less than 5 metres (16 ft.) high. Each outcrop can comprise several tiers or pillows, which may

WALKING UP ONTO THE MOORS

3. Turn left and start to walk uphill. There is no obvious path, but you are heading up to Tregarrick *Tor*. It's about a five-minute walk and the Tor will soon become visible as you climb.

4. The Tor has two distinct outcrops. Stand by the left-hand outcrop and look out across Craddock Moor. On your right, in the distance are two very tall radio masts. If you look straight ahead you will see three distinct tors on the horizon. The one on the right has a very distinct capital L shape cut out on its right-hand side. This is the Cheesewring. Head towards the left

become separated stacks: rocking pillows are called logan stones. These stacks are vulnerable to frost action and often collapse leaving trails of blocks down the slopes called clitter or clatter. Weathering has also given rise to circular "rock basins" formed by the accumulation of water and repeated freezing and thawing." (Source: Wiki)

47

of the Cheesewring aiming for between it and the middle tor. As you walk down from the Tor you will lose sight of these markers but keep walking in a straight line. As you walk across the moor, have a look out for evidence of ancient cairns and stone circles in the ground, although they can be hard to spot.

5.   Eventually, the Cheesewring will become visible again ahead of you and soon you will come to an unmade road. Turn left and walk along the road. This will take you to Gold Diggings Quarry, a perfect spot for a picnic and loved by wild swimmers. There are no fences and steep banks so you should approach the edge with care.

THE CHEESEWRING

6.   From the Quarry, return the way you came and pick a route over to the Cheesewring, the very large tor to the right. If you look at the land between you and the Cheesewring you can see some stone-fenced fields. The best route is to walk to the right of them. Head up to the top of the Cheesewring and enjoy the views.

7.   From the top of the Cheesewring look towards the two radio masts you will see a few paths below you. Coming down from the Cheesewring, you need to take the left-hand path, not the one looping around the small lake.

THE PIPERS

8.   This left-hand path is an old tramway and will take you down between all the old mine workings. Look around and you'll see old engine houses on the horizon and lots of mine shafts around you. At the bottom of the tramway step right, back onto the moor, and explore the *Craddock Moor Mine* engine house.

9.   From the side of the chimney, turn right and walk across the moor until you reach the *Hurlers* and the *Pipers*. You can't see them from the engine house, but they are only two minutes to your right. Having explored the ancient stone circles make your way towards the houses and the road. This is the village of Minions. All facilities are to the left, the walk continues right.

The Hurlers and The Pipers:
     As you look around you can see that you are standing in an area of significant Bronze Age activity. The Hurlers are a set of three granite stone circles, The Pipers are two tall pillars standing nearby. A little further away are Trethevy Quoit, Long Tom stone which we walk past, and there are also many barrows in the area. A beautiful golden cup was found in an excavated barrow at Rillaton. Recent excavations of The Hurlers show stone paths between the circles. All these Bronze Age sites so

GOLD DIGGINGS QUARRY

10. Walk alongside the road out of the village. After a while you will pass Long Tom, or the Longstone Cross, on the other side of the road. Continue along the road until you get to the cattle grid. The next short section will need to be on the road which can be busy in summer. Cross the cattle grid and walk for 200 metres until you get to a footpath sign on your right alongside the entrance to Little Barton. Walk up the drive until it veers to the left, continue straight ahead on the footpath and once it comes out on a small lane turn left.

11. Follow this lane past Great Gimble and Gimble Mill where it turns back into a footpath. At Gimble Mill the path is currently being clearly diverted for building works and may become a permanent change. Follow the local directions. Currently, this involves following the stream down to the far end of the paddock and then turning right towards a small wooden bridge.

12. Cross the bridge and walk into a field which can be a bit boggy. Walk across the field towards a large track, turn right and walk along it. Before you get to the gate at the end of the track, turn left off it and head toward the large wooden steps leading up to a bridge. Cross over and into another field.

close to each other suggests that this was a very important site.

An alternative suggestion tells the tale of a group of locals that were playing a game of hurling on the Sabbath. Hurling being a local Cornish game with a stick and ball. At the end of the day, musicians struck up a tune and the men danced and celebrated a great game. The local priest warned them not to mock the Sabbath, but they ignored him. The following day the villagers could find no trace of the hurlers or the pipers but only the stone circles and pillars.

LONG TOM AND THE CATTLE

13.   The path now lies ahead of you, following the stone wall on the right-hand side of the field. As you enter the trees take the step ladder up into the next field. Walk diagonally across this field heading uphill towards the middle pylon. Go through the gate and over into the next field. You should now be heading towards the farm buildings with the fence on your immediate left. Gradually you will see Siblyback Lake below.

14.   As you reach the farmhouse, climb over a stile. The footpath edges around the left-hand side of the farmhouse to the front of the building. Cross over the concrete drive and into the next field over another stile (currently under repair). In the field turn right and head downhill towards the next stile. This is surrounded by gorse bushes so if impassable go through the gap on its right.

15.   In this last field, head downhill at a left-hand angle, you are aiming towards the metal gate. At the bottom of the field cross over the stile and you will be back in the car park where the walk started. Full facilities are just ahead at Siblyback Lakes.

LINKS:

Mining on Craddock Moor
http://www.cornwallinfocus.co.uk/mining/craddockmoor.php
The Hurlers
http://www.readingthehurlers.co.uk/
http://www.caradonhill.org.uk/news-and-events/latest-news/98-mapping-the-sun-at -the-hurlers
Bodmin Moor
http://www.cornwall-aonb.gov.uk/bodminmoor

PHOTO ALBUM:

https://flic.kr/s/aHsmxNSa2W

8

THE COTEHELE ESTATE

This highly scenic walk takes you through woods, fields and river valleys in a hidden corner of Cornwall. As you walk, you can explore the remains of industries long gone. Large buildings lie in ruin, a water wheel still turns, and massive chimneys rise up through the woods. The walk begins and ends at a historic quay and from here it is a simple walk up to Cotehele House sitting in the middle of the walk.

LENGTH: 4 miles
EFFORT: Easy to Moderate. One steep section
TERRAIN: Footpaths, a few minor lanes
FOOTWEAR: Trainers will be fine in dry weather
LIVESTOCK: None
PARKING: Cotehele Quay (not Cotehele House). PL12 6TA
WCs: Cotehele Quay
CAFÉ / PUB: The Edgcumbe tea-room, Cotehele Quay. The Carpenter Arms, Metherell
OS MAP: 108

NEARBY ATTRACTIONS: Cotehele House, National Trust (NT). Morwellham Quay. Buckland Abbey, NT

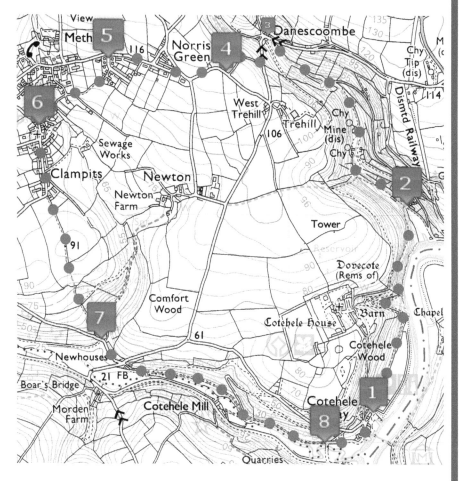

Elevation Profile

COTEHELE QUAY

DIRECTIONS:

1. Take the footpath directly behind the car park and walk into the woods, the river will be on your right. Continue along this path, ignoring any left-hand turns, for 3/4 of a mile until you get to Calstock. Along this section you will pass the 'Chapel in the Woods' and, further on, the Calstock Lookout with views over to the *Calstock Viaduct*.

2. When the path ends at a T-junction, turn left and walk along the unmade road. You will pass a sign saying, 'No Vehicular Access to Cotehele'. This sign is by a very large brick building. Further along you will pass more mining buildings. As you get to some cottages the road will turn into a footpath that crosses over a small stream. Carry on uphill until you pop out onto a tarmacked road.

Calstock Viaduct: From the Calstock Lookout viewpoint, you look down on the Tamar Valley and over to the Calstock Viaduct. Built in 1908 it is the largest viaduct in Britain to be constructed of concrete blocks and is notable for its slender proportions. The Tamar Valley itself is an Area of Outstanding Natural Beauty, with the River Tamar running all the way up from the south coast to Woolley Moor, just 3½ miles from the north coast. Just a few more miles and Cornwall would be an island.

3.   Turn left and follow the road around as it makes a sharp left-hand turn. The road now rises steeply and there is no pavement so take care. Halfway up on the right-hand side is an unmade track leading uphill. Take this right-hand turning and continue uphill. This section is steep and can be muddy. If it is too muddy you can stay on the road (look at the map) however this is the safer route. Follow the unmade track up, it turns left and then, at the top, ends at a road. This is the highest point of the walk.

4.   Having enjoyed the view and re-inserted your lungs, turn right and walk along the road. As you walk towards houses, you pass a 30mph sign, just past this there is a turning to the left, signed for Metherell and Harrowbarrow, take this turning. Walk into the village of Metherell along the pavement on the left-hand side.

CHAPEL IN THE WOODS

WALKING ALONGSIDE THE ORNAMENTAL GARDENS

5.   After a row of bungalows, turn left down Nicholas Meadow. Follow the road and as it turns left, walk forward heading downhill towards some garages. In the bottom right-hand corner of the road is a footpath with a sign pointing to Lower Metherell. Follow this path through some fields and as you leave them continue along the footpath as it edges along the high walled garden of Brooklands House. You will emerge at the bottom of a little lane. Walk uphill passing The Carpenters Arms on your right until you reach a T-junction.

6.   At the T-junction turn left and walk out of the village. As the road turns right at the end of the houses you need to take

i Cotehele Mill & Quay: There has been a mill on this site for hundreds of years. The buildings you see today were built in the nineteenth century and acted mainly to grind flour. This is still ground today, and you can buy a bag to take home and make your own bread, fresh from your walk. Following the stream downhill you pass various buildings including large lime kilns and wharfs which all serviced the once busy quay. It is now run by the National Trust but these sections of Cotehele are free to visit.

the footpath heading left at the corner. Cross the stile into a field. Walk along the clear path, following the direction of the fingerpost, and then leave the field via another stile. Take the footpath all the way downhill until you come out onto a road.

7. Turn left and follow the road until it comes to a T-junction. You need to cross straight over and walk between two stone pillars into what looks like a private drive. Follow this track all the way down to the River Morden. Walk along the footpath with the river on your right. Halfway along you can cross over the river and explore *Cotehele Mill* which has a variety of facilities. Once back on the left bank of the river continue along the path until you get to a road.

THE RIVER MORDEN

8. Walk forward and follow this road until you get to *Cotehele Quay* where you started.

LINKS:

Cotehele
https://www.nationaltrust.org.uk/cotehele

PHOTO ALBUM:

https://flic.kr/s/aHskRmXQ9e

9

LANHYDROCK HOUSE TO RESTORMEL CASTLE

A great day out, walking through the ages with lots of lovely views and important buildings. The walk starts in the grounds of Lanhydrock and then heads through the woods and river down to the Bodmin Parkway railway station. It then continues down to Restormel Castle. From the castle, it's an easy walk back to the Lanhydrock Estate.

ADDITIONAL INFORMATION: Restormel Castle is only open seasonally. If you wish to visit, check the link at the end of this walk.

LENGTH: 8½ miles
EFFORT: Moderate to challenging, simply due to length and hills
TERRAIN: Lanes, cycle paths, footpaths
FOOTWEAR: Walking boots, trainers
LIVESTOCK: Sheep
PARKING: Lanhydrock National Trust car park. PL30 5AD
WCs: Lanhydrock / Duchy Nurseries / Bodmin Parkway station
CAFÉ / PUB: Lanhydrock / Duchy Nurseries
OS MAP: 107

NEARBY ATTRACTIONS: Lostwithiel. Lanhydrock House, National Trust. Restormel Castle, English Heritage

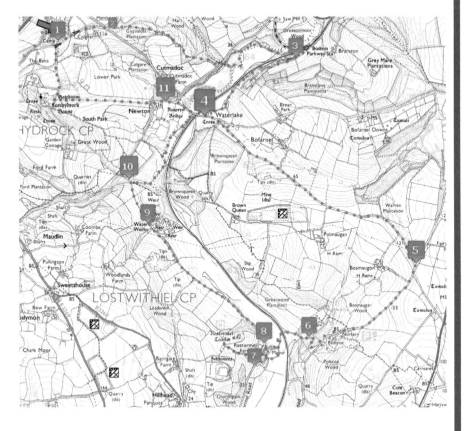

Elevation Profile

330ft						
160ft						
0.0mi	1.2mi	2.5mi	3.7mi	5.0mi	6.2mi	7.5mi	**8.7mi**

FRIENDLY LOCALS

DIRECTIONS:

1. Park in the *Lanhydrock Estate* main car park. Head towards the house, and as you leave the car park you will come to a road. Instead of crossing it towards the house, turn left and walk up the road with the cricket pavilion on your left. At the T-junction, cross the road and enter the woods. You are now on a large unmade road, this is a very popular cycle trails area so keep an eye out for lots of bikes. Head forwards and take the right-hand path leading downhill. This will have a National Trust post with a green oak leaf, a yellow arrow and a no bikes sign.

i **Lanhydrock Estate:** Lanhydrock is the perfect country house and estate, with the feel of a wealthy but unpretentious family home. After a devastating fire in 1881, the Jacobean house was refurbished in high-Victorian style, with the best in country house design, planning and all the latest mod-cons. Beyond the house, the gardens and further estate grounds are beautiful to explore, and this walk winds through a lot of them

2.   It is about a 10 / 15 minutes walk downhill. When you get to the bottom head through the gate, cross the road and into the Lanhydrock Estate grounds. Cross over the formal path and take the path following the stream; keep it on your right and walk down to the river. When you get there, turn left and follow it upriver. The path rejoins the formal path and turns right. Walk between the metal railings, over the river and continue all the way to Bodmin Parkway railway station.

free of charge. The newly developed cycle trails are also worth exploring. Dating from the seventeenth century, the main gatehouse escaped the ravages of the fire. This makes it one of the few remaining features of the previous great house.

LANHYDROCK GATEHOUSE

3.   As you walk into the car park, you need to turn sharp right towards an industrial estate. When you get to the gates for the estate, stay on the drive as it veers to the right. The road becomes increasingly unmade, as you get halfway along the very long building on your left you need to take an unsigned footpath to your right. This heads straight down to the railway line and you will walk past some storage buildings on your right. At the railway line turn left and walk along the path. Go through a five-bar gate and continue until you get to a kissing-gate. Once through this you are now walking through a private garden. Head towards their drive and then walk along it away from the house, all the way to the road.

4.   At the road, turn left. Start walking uphill, take the right-hand turning to Lostwithiel and continue walking uphill. Eventually, the road turns right to the 'Duchy of Cornwall Nursery and Café'. This whole section, from where the path joins the road to the Duchy turning is about 1½ miles. As you walk under the pylon lines, you are just about at the turning. This is a quiet road with lovely high views.

(i) **Respryn Bridge:**
Respryn Bridge is a five-arched mediaeval bridge spanning the River Fowey in the parish of Lanhydrock. The place name indicates a ford here before the bridge was built, carrying an ancient trackway between Bodmin and Looe: traces of which have been identified as a hollow way running north-westwards through Cutmadoc and Colgear Plantation in Lanhydrock Park.

Documentary evidence indicates a chapel of St Martin, on the St Winnow side of the river in the twelfth century. This predated the bridge and served the fording point. By 1300, however, there was a bridge here.

(i) **Restormel Castle:**
"The great thirteenth century circular shell-keep of Restormel still encloses the principal rooms of the castle in remarkably good condition. It stands on an earlier Norman mound surrounded by a deep dry ditch, atop a high spur beside the River Fowey. Twice visited by the Black Prince, it finally saw action during the Civil War in 1644. It commands fantastic views and is a favourite picnic spot.

5.   At the turning, head right, this lane is much smaller and finally downhill. As you look to your right across the valley, you can see *Restormel Castle* nestling on the hillside. Continue down the lane until you get to the driveway for the Duchy Nurseries. Take the footpath opposite the driveway on your right. Go through the small gate marked 'EH Restormel Castle'. The path zigzags all the way downhill and is well signed.

When you visit, keep an eye out for 'Tetraphasis Obscurus', the 'Black Pheasant' that you can spot in the castle grounds and nearby woodland. This is a haven for wildlife and birds with beautiful spring flowers and plants all year round." English Heritage

RESTORMEL CASTLE

6.   At the bottom go through the five-bar gate and follow the path, crossing over the railway bridge and then over the river bridge as well. Go through another gate and then follow the path as it skirts around *Restormel Manor*. Go through the next gate and then walk towards the estate buildings until you get to a T-junction. Step 7 offers a fascinating detour otherwise go to Step 8.

7.   If you want to visit the castle, turn left and follow the signs, returning to this point afterwards. It is very impressive, being a beautiful example of a circular castle, but is only opened seasonally. Having explored, return to the T-junction.

8.   At the T-junction turn right. Pass the *Duchy of Cornwall* estate office car park, and stick to the road for the next mile, this is flat and very quiet. When it bears sharp left, go through the gate and carry on walking forward on the road. This will make more sense when you see it.

9.   Walk past the water treatment centre and continue on as the road turns into a track in a field. Continue through the field until you get to the maroon gate. Pass through and you are now back on the Lanhydrock Estate.

10.   Turn right and head down towards the river. When you get to the river, turn left and follow it upstream until you get to a footbridge. Cross over the river and continue upstream until you get to the road.

Restormel Manor:
Restormel Manor is approximately 500 years old and sits on the site of the ancient Holy Trinity Chapel. It is still owned and operated by the *Duchy of Cornwall*. The manor itself now acts as private holiday accommodation and is often used by the Royal family when visiting the area.

Duchy of Cornwall:
Along with Lancashire, Cornwall is the only duchy remaining in Britain. The Duke of Cornwall is also the Prince of Wales and heir to the British throne. Unlike Lancashire, the Cornish Duchy has developed historically, unusual legal amendments have created a special position within the UK. In 2014, the UK government announced that *"the proud history, unique culture, and distinctive language of Cornwall will be fully recognised under European rules for the protection of national minorities"*.

RESTORMEL MANOR

11. Turn left onto the road and cross over *Respryn Bridge*, walk past the car park on your right and then take the left-hand turning up to Lanhydrock House. Follow this path through the first gatehouse and up the ornamental drive right up to the very ornate main gatehouse. Turn right before this second *gatehouse* and follow the road uphill. This leads back to your car park.

LINKS:

Duchy Nurseries Opening Times
http://www.duchyofcornwallnursery.co.uk/
Lanhydrock – National Trust
https://www.nationaltrust.org.uk/lanhydrock
Respryn Bridge
http://bit.ly/2HXf7V9
Restormel Castle
http://bit.ly/2GbrrUK

PHOTO ALBUM:

https://flic.kr/s/aHsmeDgEFW

10

GRIBBIN HEAD AND THE SAINTS' WAY

An excellent walk combining the Coast Path and the Saints' Way this is a nice circular loop with great views. Much of this walk is the setting for Rebecca by Daphne du Maurier. Along the way, you will also pass the Gribbin Daymark, the tall, red and white iconic tower.

ADDITIONAL INFORMATION: This is a very popular route and can become quite churned up after heavy rain. The Gribbin Daymark is often open one day a week, during summer. It is well worth visiting as you can climb all the way to the top and the views are spectacular. Dogs not allowed. Details are in the link at the end of the walk.

OPTIONAL WALK: This walk can be linked with the *Lankelly Loop* walk.

LENGTH: 5 miles
EFFORT: Moderate
TERRAIN: Coast Path, fields and lanes
FOOTWEAR: Trainers. Boots when muddy
LIVESTOCK: Some cattle, and you do walk through a farmyard
PARKING: Coombe Farm National Trust car park. PL23 1HW
WCs: Steep diversion off the path to Polkerris
CAFÉ / PUB: Small but steep diversion off the path to Polkerris
OS MAP: 107

NEARBY ATTRACTIONS: Fowey. The Eden Project. Restormel Castle, English Heritage

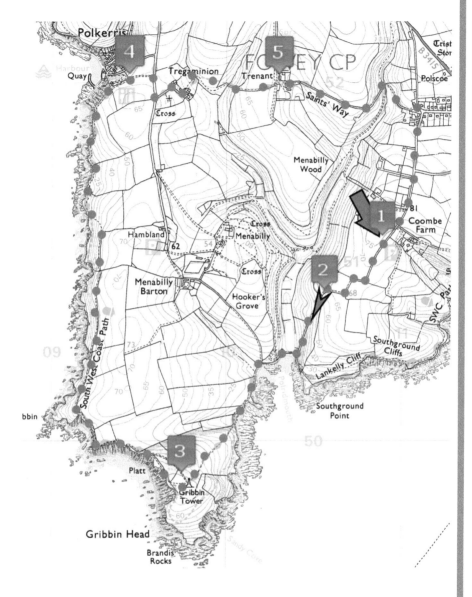

Elevation Profile

260ft								
200ft								
130ft								
66ft								

0.0mi   0.62mi   1.2mi   1.9mi   2.5mi   3.1mi   3.7mi   4.4mi   **4.9mi**

WALKING ALONG THE SAINTS' WAY

DIRECTIONS:

1. Go through the small five-bar gate in the corner of the car park and turn left down the footpath. Follow the path until it ends at a large five-bar gate. Go through the gate into the field and turn left. Walk along the edge of the field, pass the first gate and at the second gate, go through and back onto a clear path.

2. Follow the path all the way down to Polridmouth Beach. The house by the beach was the inspiration for the boat-house in Daphne du Maurier's *Rebecca* (see notes in the Lankelly Loop Walk). At the bottom, turn right, you are now on the Coast Path and will stay on this path for the next 2½ miles. As you leave Polridmouth Beach, the path starts to climb steeply up to the *Gribbin Daymark*,

Gribbin Daymark:
"Erected by Trinity House 'for the safety of commerce and the preservation of mariners' the tower pinpoints the approach to Fowey's narrow and rocky harbour entrance. This meant that sailors did not mistake the treacherous shallows of St Austell Bay for the deep waters of Falmouth harbour." National Trust.

Its decorative design is down to the request of the Rashleigh landowners. If you compare it to the Daymark at Stepper Point in Walk 5 *Padstow to Stepper Point* you will see that this is a most impressive version.

this is the toughest part of the walk, but the views at the top are spectacular.

3. Continue along the Coast Path but be aware the path is very high up here and at times, close to the edge, so keep dogs on leads. Eventually, the path heads inland above Polkerris. This is a lovely place to stop and explore and has WCs but it's quite a walk down to it, and of course back up to this point. The Coast Path turns sharp left and downhill towards Polkerris, but this is where we leave it. Our path continues across the middle of a field, although not always signed, the path is usually clear to see on the ground itself, head towards the telegraph pole. We are now walking along *the Saints' Way*.

The Saints' Way: During the early spread of Christianity from Ireland and the Scottish communities, there was a lot of traffic along the western edge of the British Isles. Saints travelled between Scotland, Ireland, Wales, Cornwall and Brittany. There is evidence all over Cornwall of the impact that the saints had on the land; there are more saint place names in Cornwall than anywhere else in Britain. These holy men and women were clearly passing through Cornwall and whilst an actual path was never known, one could be guessed at. In the late 1990s, a Saints' Way across Cornwall, connecting important religious sites from the fifth century, was established. Of course, it wouldn't have just been Saints using these paths. Cornwall was rich in tin, which had fuelled the Bronze Age and there is evidence of the tin trade stretching as far as the Phoenician trading routes. Ireland and Wales were also rich in gold so there would have been many merchants. One story claims that Joseph of Arimathea came to Cornwall to trade in tin and that one of his companions was Jesus

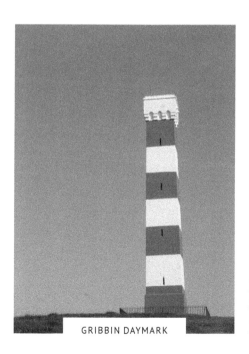

GRIBBIN DAYMARK

4. At the road, turn right, walk 100 metres along the road and then turn left at *Tregaminion Church*. The churchyard features two *wayside crosses* moved here by William Rashleigh. Now walk down the lane into the farmyard; the path is clearly marked and heads right through the middle of the farmyard. From the farmyard, head into the field, through the gate on your left. Walk down to the footbridge and cross over it into another field. Follow the path until you cross a rickety footbridge and then climb a large flight of steps.

himself. Whilst the legitimacy of this claim is weak, the fact that the story exists lends evidence to the importance of Cornwall, as a place of great resources and international trading for the last two thousand years.

i **Tregaminion Church & the Wayside Crosses:** Tregaminion Church was begun in 1813 by William Rashleigh, it is now a Chapel of

THE SETTING FOR *REBECCA*

5. The path comes to a sheep stile (stone steps in the wall) and crosses a small lane. Go straight over and continue along the path between the buildings. Walk further until you reach another sheep stile and head straight down the old lane, under a bridge, through a kissing-gate and then over a small stream. Now follow the path right and uphill until you emerge onto Prickly Post Lane. Once on the lane, turn right and stick to this road all the way back to your car park.

HIDDEN PATHWAYS

LINKS:

Gribbin Daymark
https://bit.ly/2pAFf0M
Large wayside cross
https://bit.ly/2pxXDbk
Small wayside cross
https://bit.ly/2pB7nRr

PHOTO ALBUM:

https://flic.kr/s/aHskwB2GXG

Ease and rarely open. In its grounds stand two wayside crosses that would have acted as route markers. Just as we follow the fingerposts today, these crosses provided markers for ancient traders and pilgrims. The first, standing by the front porch, is believed to have been moved here sometime in the nineteenth century, possibly from the road outside. The second, larger cross, standing almost complete and off to the side amongst the trees, has had an eventful journey. In the words of Historic England, "*This wayside cross was discovered in 1889 in use as part of a footbridge across a stream at Milltown in Lanlivery parish, 6km north of Tregaminion. The head had been reshaped so that it would lie flat against another stone. The monks of Buckfast Abbey, Devon bought the cross for five pounds and moved it to Buckfast. When the landowner, William Rashleigh of Menabilly, heard about the cross, he claimed it and had it re-erected in the chapel yard at Tregaminion, in its present location.*"

11

LANKELLY LOOP

An enjoyable, short walk with great sea views and popular with dog walkers. There is the opportunity to explore a small Tudor castle and visit the sites that were the inspiration for Rebecca by Daphne du Maurier.

ADDITIONAL INFORMATION: This is a very popular route and can become quite churned up after heavy rain.

OPTIONAL WALK: This walk can be linked with the *Gribbin Head* walk.

LENGTH: 2½ miles
EFFORT: Moderate
TERRAIN: Fields and Coast Path
FOOTWEAR: Trainers. Boots when muddy
LIVESTOCK: Cattle sometimes on the Coast Path
PARKING: Coombe Farm National Trust car park. PL23 1HW. It is possible to join this walk from Fowey, have a look at the map
WCs: None
CAFÉ / PUB: None
OS MAP: 107

NEARBY ATTRACTIONS: Fowey. The Eden Project. Restormel Castle, English Heritage

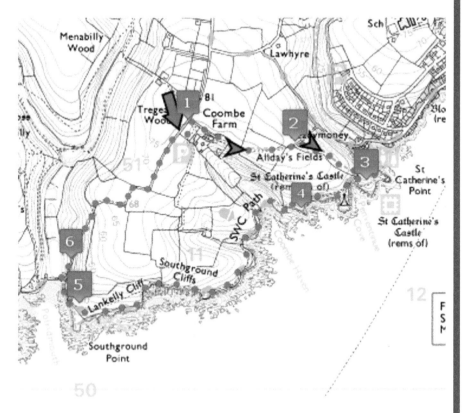

Elevation Profile

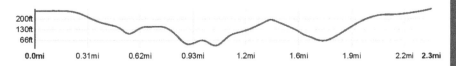

ST CATHERINE'S CASTLE

DIRECTIONS:

1. From the Coombe Farm National Trust car park, head back towards the road and take the footpath to Coombe Haven. There is a clear fingerpost pointing the way. At the end of the lane go through the five-bar gate and into a field. Walk across the field taking the more distinctive path veering left. Walk into the second field and then turn left towards the trees and a black, metal kissing-gate.

2. Go through the gate and into the woods. After about 10 yards take the smaller path on the right and follow it down through the woods. It levels

St Catherine's Castle: Built in 1538 by Henry VIII to protect Fowey from the threat of a French invasion, it was later modified to house two guns during the Crimean War, and later again, more guns were installed during the Second World War. There is no evidence that the castle defences were ever actually deployed in combat.

out for a bit and then turns left and downhill again, where it stops at the foundations of an old building. Take the steps to the left and head down to a larger footpath. Turn right onto this path and walk towards the English Heritage signpost for *St Catherine's Castle*.

If you are walking with dogs, make sure they are on a short lead around the castle. Explore the castle and then return to the English Heritage signpost.

3.   Turn right, back the way you came, and then turn left and immediately turn sharp left and climb a small, steep path up towards the *Rashleigh Mausoleum*. After you have had a look around, head back down to the path, then turn left and walk up to a wooden gate. You are now on the Coast Path and will stick to this for the next mile.

i **The Rashleigh Family:** This section of Cornwall is utterly dominated by the Rashleigh Estate. Whether it's Point Neptune, the Mausoleum, Gribbin Daymark, the village of Polkerris, Charlestown Docks (just beyond this walk), Menabilly, the Rashleigh Inn, or the Waymarker Crosses; the Rashleighs have built it, owned it or developed it. The family rose to power and riches in the Tudor period, settled in the Fowey area, and were no doubt instrumental in the sacking and reallocation of the Tywardreath Priory wealth. They grew their wealth in shipping and mining, and by 1873 Jonathan Rashleigh was the largest landowner in Cornwall.

THE HIDDEN RASHLEIGH MONUMENT

4.   In the distance is a large red and white tower, this is the Gribbin Daymark. We are walking towards it but won't actually walk to it. Dogs can happily roam along this section, but after you pass Coombe Haven, you will go through a gate warning about cattle. The next three fields might have cattle in them, so dogs on leads until you are certain. The Coast Path also runs close to cliffs so again, dogs on leads. In the third field, it is easy to see if there are any cattle and the path heads inland, away from the cliffs and towards the woods.

Rebecca by Daphne du Maurier:
"*Last night I dreamt I went to Manderley again.*" Hidden in the woods, behind the ornamental lake stands Menabilly House, the Rashleigh ancestral home, that serves as the inspiration for Manderley in *Rebecca*. When du Maurier first discovered the house, it was neglected and probably most resembled the wreck that it

VIEW BACK INTO FOWEY HARBOUR

5.   The path now heads into the trees and sharply downhill to Polridmouth Beach. As you walk down, you can see a house sitting by a large ornamental lake. This was the inspiration for the boathouse in *Rebecca* by *Daphne du Maurier*.

6.   As you reach the beach take the right-hand footpath heading uphill. This section is long and steep, but when you get to the top, you can enjoy the views back down to the sea. Go through the gate and turn right. Follow along the right-hand edge of the field, turn left at the corner of the field and head towards the wooden gate. Pass through the gate, onto the track and follow it until you return to your car park.

becomes in her book. *Rebecca* is a sinister, dark novel but it is also a paean to a house. Happily, a few years later she was able to lease Menabilly from the Rashleigh family, restoring it to its former glory, and lived there for 26 years.

LINKS:

Daphne du Maurier
https://bit.ly/2DQdsyq
Rashleigh Mausoleum
https://bit.ly/2BUN2in
St Catherine's Castle
https://bit.ly/2G31gMM

PHOTO ALBUM:

https://flic.kr/s/aHskwdbi5G

12

LOOE, DULOE AND A TRAIN RIDE

The best sort of walk includes a chance to put your feet up. This route travels through woodland, along the ancient Giant's Hedge, some tiny lanes and then alongside a stream before heading uphill to Duloe, home to Cornwall's smallest stone circle and a very fine pub. Finally, enjoy a very scenic train ride back to Looe.

ADDITIONAL INFORMATION: Check the *train timetables*. Potential for flooding. Great for dogs.

LENGTH: 6½ miles, excluding the train ride
EFFORT: Moderate – one very steep section
TERRAIN: Woodland trails. Some minor lanes
FOOTWEAR: Trainers will be fine in dry weather
LIVESTOCK: None
PARKING: Millpool car park. PL13 2AH
WCs: Looe. Duloe
CAFÉ / PUB: The Plough, Duloe
OS MAP: 107

NEARBY ATTRACTIONS: St George's Island. Cornish Orchards Cider Farm

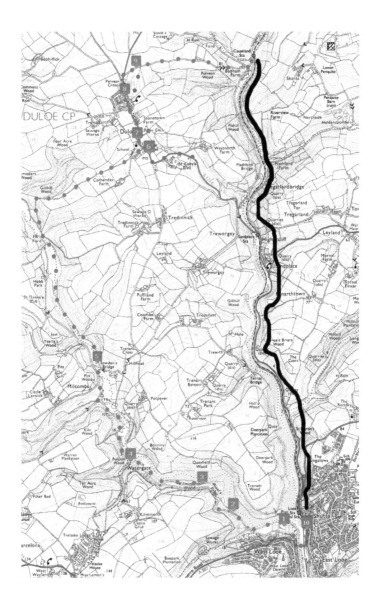

Elevation Profile

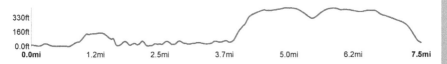

330ft						
160ft						
0.0ft						
0.0mi	1.2mi	2.5mi	3.7mi	5.0mi	6.2mi	7.5mi

TAKING THE TRAIN HOME

DIRECTIONS:

1. In the Millpool car park head towards the water. Turn left onto the footpath and keep on this path until the end of the car park. At the end, turn right and head up towards the Kilminorth Woods.

2. Head through the gate and from the fingerpost take the 'Riverside and Watergate' path. When the path splits take the left-hand fork heading uphill towards 'Watergate 1½'. When the path turns sharply right, there is a collection

Giant's Hedge:
The Giant's Hedge is an earthwork stretching from Looe to Lerryn. It's believed to be post-Roman and there are suggestions that it was built by King Mark to protect his kingdom. This is only supposition, but it is manmade and whilst it is no longer so obvious, it was once a massive structure following a natural rise in the land. In parts,

of wooden steps and bridges, walk up the small flight of steps in front of you and turn right along the smaller path. You are now walking along the edge of the *Giant's Hedge*.

3.　At the next fingerpost turn right and head down to the larger footpath, then turn left and continue along. When you reach a crossroad, take the right-hand path marked 'Alternate Return Route'. This is a steep flight of steps down to the river and can be slippery. At the bottom, turn left.

the hedge is about 5 metres high and 3 metres wide. It would have been very difficult to attack. The more enjoyable folklore rhyme says, *"Jack the giant had nothing to do, so he made a hedge from Lerryn to Looe."*

LENDING LIBRARY

4.   Follow along the river path until you head out through a small gate and into the pretty setting of Watergate. Head towards the houses and turn right onto a little lane. Halfway along you will pass a lime kiln on your left and a ford to your right. Continue until the road ends at a T-junction. Turn right and walk until you cross over the river. Just after the bridge is a footpath to the left. Take this path (after very heavy rains it may be too flooded in which case stay on the road walking up into Duloe).

5.   The path takes you along the West Looe River. There are several stiles along this section of the walk. The path is obvious but there are yellow footpath signs along the way, at one section it heads up into a field but then returns down to the river. The path eventually ends at a junction. Ignore the track to your immediate right, heading roughly back the way you came. Instead, cross over the stile to your left, cross over the stream and then take the track heading uphill. At the point that the track splits take the right-hand fork and walk up towards Duloe. You may want to briefly pause, make a will and then head on up. Near the top, the track becomes a small tarmacked road, recover your breath and then continue along until you get to a T-junction. You are now in Duloe, by the church. Step 6 offers a fascinating detour otherwise go to Step 7.

St Cuby Holy Well: This is a very pretty well house, hiding under trees beside the road. The well house is large enough to enter and there are two stone benches before the second chamber that houses the well. It's a really tranquil spot and a lovely place to sit and rest a while.

ST CUBY HOLY WELL

6.   There is a very pretty *holy well* a half mile away. To visit it, turn right at the T-junction following the signs to the Cornish Orchards. Just before Duloe Manor Holiday complex, there is a gate on the right-hand side of the road. It leads to a very pretty glade you may wish to visit. Otherwise, continue past Duloe Manor, the footpath ends here and I would recommend crossing to the other side of the busy road so that you can be seen better. Just after the turning to the Cornish Orchards, the well can be found tucked into the right-hand side of the road. Having enjoyed this very calm spot, return to Duloe Church.

7.   Turn left at the T-junction and head into the village. As you walk there is a signpost pointing right towards the *Duloe Stone Circle*. Head down the path into the field to explore and then return to the road and continue right. There are usually sheep in this field. If you stop at the pub for food, I would give yourself about 30 minutes to get from here to the train station.

8.   To get to the train, walk out of the village in the direction of Liskeard, this small section is without a pavement and can be busy. Take the small unmarked lane on the right, just past the national speed limit signs. Alternatively, take the footpath by the public loos, this path cuts across an arable field and will drop out onto the lane. It cuts off a corner but is very claggy in wet weather.

Duloe Stone Circle: This is Cornwall's smallest stone circle and is often overlooked, which is a shame as it's lovely. It comprises eight large, white quartz stones in a field that usually has livestock in it. There is evidence that this may have been a burial site with the stones forming a peristalith, an outer ring making a Bronze Age barrow.

9.   The lane heading down to Causeland is tiny and barely used by cars, towards the end it becomes very steep as it drops down to the valley floor. At the bottom, turn left and follow the signs to the train platform. You will need to flag the train down as it approaches as it will not stop otherwise. Sit on the right-hand side for the best views.

10.   When you arrive back in Looe you will need to turn right and cross over the large road bridge to return to the start of the walk. Just over the river take the little road that drops to the right and this will head back into the car park.

DULOE STONE CIRCLE

LINKS:

Causeland Stop for Duloe - Train Timetable
https://greatscenicrailways.co.uk/lines/looe-valley-line/
History of Duloe and St Cuby
https://www.stcubyduloe.org.uk/welcome-to-st-cuby-in-duloe/history/
Duloe Stone Circle
http://www.historic-cornwall.org.uk/a2m/bronze_age/stone_circle/duloe/duloe.htm

PHOTO ALBUM:

https://flic.kr/s/aHsmxNQpuC

13

MOUNT EDGCUMBE

A beautiful and varied walk through the Edgcumbe Estate. Starting in the formal gardens with views over to Plymouth, the walk heads into the woods with views out to sea. The path then turns inland across the parkland before heading back to the car.

ADDITIONAL INFORMATION: There are several free leaflets which describe some of the features along the walk. Collect these from any of the information points before you set off.

OPTIONAL WALK: There is a lovely 4-mile simple circular cliff top walk on the Rame Head. Parking at Cawsand.

LENGTH: 4 miles
EFFORT: Moderate
TERRAIN: Coast Path, paved tracks, fields
FOOTWEAR: Trainers will be fine in dry weather
LIVESTOCK: Some potential for sheep
PARKING: Mount Edgcumbe
WCs: Mount Edgcumbe
CAFÉ / PUB: The Orangery Garden Café, Mount Edgcumbe. The Canteen at Maker Heights
OS MAP: 108

NEARBY ATTRACTIONS: Plymouth via Ferry. Antony. Antony Woodland Gardens, National Trust. Rame Head

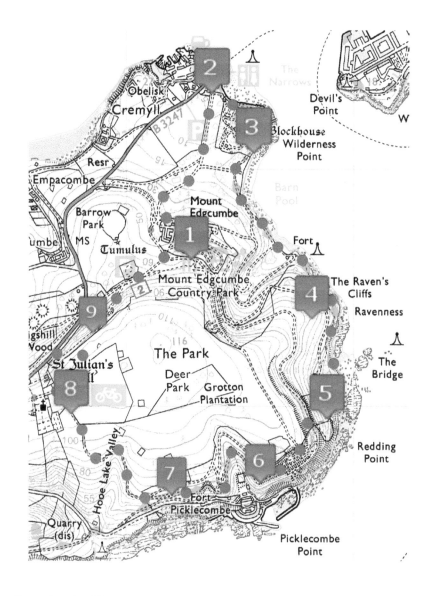

Elevation Profile

330ft

160ft

0.0mi   0.62mi   1.2mi   1.9mi   2.5mi   3.1mi   **3.5mi**

FORMAL GARDENS

DIRECTIONS:

1. From the car park make your way down between the out-buildings to the front of *Mount Edgcumbe House*. Standing at the front of the house, with glorious views down over Plymouth, turn left and walk along the main drive towards the colonnaded pineapples. Walk down beside the pine-apples to see the icehouse. Then walk down across the lawn heading towards the drive. Once you reach the drive follow it downhill and then take the left-hand fork continuing down to the Orangery and formal gardens.

i **Plymouth Naval Sites:** Looking across the water it is clear to see the naval importance of Plymouth. On this side of the water you will also pass military features, but the main thrust of the Navy is across the water and on the small islands in Plymouth Sound. See if you can also spot Plymouth Breakwater Fort a long barrier out in the mouth of the Sound. Plymouth has had a very long and strategic role in British maritime

2.   At the bottom of the drive head through the large stone pillars and you may wish to explore Cremyll. Across the water, you are looking at Plymouth and her many *naval sites*. Once done head back into the Edgcumbe Estate and turn left into the Orangery gardens. Walk up the left-hand flight of ornate steps opposite the Orangery and into the formal gardens. Veer left, towards the apiary and explore the beautiful gardens. Gradually, make your way back down to the path alongside the sea. There are many paths through and exits from the gardens, so history. The Pilgrim Fathers sailed from Plymouth to America on the Mayflower, Francis Drake set sail from here to defeat the Spanish Armada, when Napoleon was captured in 1815, he was briefly held at Plymouth and Hitler targeted and destroyed much of Plymouth during WW2. HMNB Devonport is the largest naval base in Western Europe and has been supporting the Royal Navy since 1691. The vast site

AZALEAS

long as you head back to the sea it will be fine.

3.   The path follows a sea wall and then a beach, depending on which point you exit the formal gardens. Turn right, passing the beach and then take the left-hand fork leading uphill, this is signposted towards the Amphitheatre. The path leads up into trees and then opens onto a lawned area with a large pond, this section is known as the Amphitheatre. Head towards a white Palladian folly temple. As you pass the temple the footpath heads up into the wilder area of the estate and

covers more than 650 acres and has 15 dry docks, 4 miles of waterfront, 25 tidal berths and five basins. The base employs 2,500 service personnel and civilians, supports around 400 local firms and generates around 10% of Plymouth's income.

A GARDEN FULL OF ART

you are now on the Coast Path. The path is no longer paved but remains wide and firm. As you reach the parkland there is a gate requesting that all dogs should be put on leads.

4. Once through the gate, turn right and head up to a lovely ruined folly. The path is steep, but the views are fabulous. From the folly retrace your steps back down the hill and then turn right. The path now heads into woodland.

5. Walk along the path until you reach a long flight of steps. These head up to the Red Seat and more spectacular views. As you get to the Red Seat, ignore the large path leading right into the fields but continue along the smaller Coast Path. Shortly after the Red Seat, on your left are the Zigzags, lots of small decorative steps, you can go down and explore them as they soon re-join the Coast Path.

6. Continue along the Coast Path until it appears to bear sharp right. Ignore this and make sure you follow the Coast Path signs heading left, downhill. Below you may see tennis courts and Fort Pilkington. Continue along the path as it by-passes the private fort. There is a pretty, converted seat ideally placed to enjoy the view. This is the Picklecombe Seat and was built using a mediaeval arch and other stone from nearby churches.

ONE OF THE MANY FOLLIES

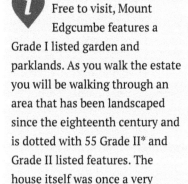

VIEW OVER TO PLYMOUTH

7.   Continuing along, the path forks and you need to leave the Coast Path by taking the right-hand path. When you get to a five-bar gate go through and continue along the main path that veers to the right. The path gradually turns to grass as you head up on the right-hand side of a long valley that runs down to the sea. Continue uphill to the top of this valley. Gradually the path climbs uphill towards a church ahead on the left.

i **Mount Edgcumbe:** Free to visit, Mount Edgcumbe features a Grade I listed garden and parklands. As you walk the estate you will be walking through an area that has been landscaped since the eighteenth century and is dotted with 55 Grade II* and Grade II listed features. The house itself was once a very

8.   Keep the church car park on your left and follow the fence all the way down the hill until you get to a stile. Cross over and a holy well should be just below. Having explored, return back over the stile and walk uphill bearing left until you meet a clear grass path. Turn left onto the path and walk down to the gate.

9.   On the other side of the gate follow the track downhill until it meets a road. Turn right and walk along the road, when the road forks, take the right-hand fork. Follow this road until it makes a sharp left-hand U-turn, make the turn then turn immediately right following the road down between the two wooden picket fences. You are now at the top end of the car park.

important building being the home of The Earls of Edgcumbe. It was begun in 1547 and mostly destroyed by fire in 1941, during a bombing raid. However, a large section remains and can be visited for a fee.

LINKS:

A History of Plymouth
https://www.oneplymouth.co.uk/plymouths-history-a-step-back-in-time/
The Edgcumbe Family
https://thatsmycornwall.com/the-great-families-of-cornwall-the-edgcumbes/

PHOTO ALBUM:

https://flic.kr/s/aHsmbZ2urZ

EXTRA HELPINGS

I SPY

CELTIC CROSS

In some spots of Cornwall, you could trip over these, there are so many. They come in all shapes and guises but very few are a straight cross shape. In the past, they were moved around a lot and were also re-used as footbridges, foundation stones or gate posts, as well as cattle rubs.

GRANITE TOR

Weather erosion has created these incredible structures on the top of some hills. These are strangely shaped boulders, perching on top of each other. Bonus points if you find one with a Logan Stone. This is a rock that rocks and pivots when you stand on it.

WIND TURBINE

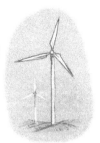

Over the past few years, these giant white turbines have popped up all over the landscape.

DRIES

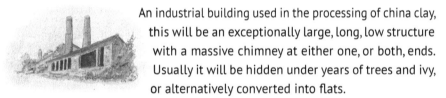

An industrial building used in the processing of china clay, this will be an exceptionally large, long, low structure with a massive chimney at either one, or both, ends. Usually it will be hidden under years of trees and ivy, or alternatively converted into flats.

ENGINE HOUSE

A tall upright building with a massive chimney on one side. Easily spotted due to their isolation and height. Engine houses are most commonly associated with tin mines, they were used to pump water out of the shafts below ground. Some of the mines even run below the seabed.

CASTLE

We have several castles in Cornwall and most of them seem to be round. As well as Mediaeval and Tudor castles we also have ancient hillforts and strongholds, including Tintagel, the suggested birthplace of King Arthur.

LIGHTHOUSE

Some of our lighthouses were built simply as automated lights, some however, were once occupied. The Lizard Lighthouse was the last one to remain manned and was only switched to an automated system in 1998. Many have now been turned into holiday homes.

CHOUGH

Easily distinguished by their bright red beaks and feet, and their aerobatics Cornwall's national bird can be found mainly on the cliffs to the west of the county. At one point they disappeared from our shores altogether and only recently has a group started to re-colonise the county to the extent that they are now starting to spread slowly but surely east.

BUZZARD

A large brown, bird of prey often mistaken for an eagle, but we don't have any of them. If you see crows or gulls mobbing a larger bird it will probably be a buzzard. Keep an eye out for telegraph poles as they like to perch there.

MUSSELS

One of nature's natural bounties and the easiest shellfish to identify with their long blue-black oval cases. Archaeological records show that we have been eating mussels for the past 20,000 years.

CRAB

Fresh or on the fish stand, either will do. A popular summer activity is crabbing from a harbour wall, although you will never catch a crab large enough to eat. Get a line with a hook on the end and pierce on a bit of bacon, drop it in the water. Lo and behold, a few minutes later you'll have hooked a crab. Have a look, then throw it back in the sea.

SEAWEED

Well, what's the fun in not having an easy one to spot? Most seaweed is actually edible, in fact, several places in Cornwall now have it on the menu. Order some, it's really tasty.

SEAL

Like cows and dogs, seals are friendly and curious. They often come into harbours for easy food and to have a nose about. Out on coastal walks, they will often pop up if they hear new sounds. They seem to like listening to singing.

FOXGLOVE

These lovely tall pink spires herald early summer and grow wild across Cornwall. The Cornish hedgerows are a sight to behold in spring, although you wouldn't want to bump into one as they are actually granite walls wrapped in earth and plants.

SURFBOARD

We've been surfing in Cornwall ever since St Piran arrived in Cornwall, surfing in on a millstone, from Ireland. Surfing gained mass appeal at the beginning of the twentieth century using boogie boards or belly boards. It didn't take long before people switched over to standing up on much larger boards. Bonus points if you spot an old-style wooden boogie board.

FISHING BOAT

Another easy spot but see if you can identify some of the registrations. FY means the vessel was registered in Fowey. PW is Padstow, PZ is Penzance, SC is the Scilly Isles, SS is St Ives and FH is Falmouth. Bonus points for TO, which is Truro.

CORNISH LANGUAGE

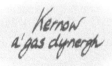

The best place to spot this is on road signs but have a look around, you'll find it in all sorts of places. The language died out in 1770 but following a concerted effort, there are now several hundred Cornish speakers, although as yet, there are no native speakers. Give it time.

PASTY

A shy beast and often misrepresented. In the past, a pasty was a worker's lunch and was filled with whatever was to hand, including fish or fruit. Today, a traditional pasty is filled with steak, taken from the skirt cut of beef, swede, potatoes, onion, salt, butter and pepper. Nothing else. It must also be crimped on the side, not over the top. The pasty has even got a protected specialist status, detailing these features.

WHAT TO DO IN CORNWALL WHEN IT RAINS

A light-hearted guide

You've booked a week off, you've been looking forward to it for ages, the kids are excited, the weather is sunny, and you are making great time down the M5 but wait, what's that ahead of you? Is it seven days of sea, sand and sunshine or is it a dirty big cloud looming over the Devon / Cornwall border? Honestly, I don't know why people don't just stop in Devon, it's closer, it's larger, it's, oh who am I kidding, it's NOT Cornwall. Anyway, you drive on, confident that one cloud can't cover a whole county for a whole entire week.

Welcome to Cornwall. Or *Kernow a'gas dynergh* which means it always rains here.[1] But a week of rain doesn't have to mean the end of the world. Especially if you plan ahead.

STEP ONE: DON'T CAMP

Only camp if a) you are a seasoned camper or b) it won't kill you if you have to pack up and go home early. Otherwise, don't do it. Camping is for a rare breed of people, let's call them sadists or psychopaths. I will hold my hand up here and declare an extreme bias.[2]

STEP TWO: PACK FOR WINTER AND YOU'LL BE FINE

I mean, by all means, pack for summer as well but there is nothing more miserable than shivering around Trago in your Hawaiian short-sleeve top and your cargo shorts or pulling on damp clothes in the morning. Also, pack your wellies. It is a fact that every single person in Cornwall owns a pair of wellies,[3] in fact after our flip flops it's the second most popular footwear of choice. Because of course when it isn't raining it's glorious here. That's why you are unloading your car, in a downpour.

STEP THREE: YOU'VE ARRIVED

You are not under canvas and you have proper clothing and footwear. Honestly, that's most of the problem fixed, because you are here, in the best place in Britain and you are properly prepared.

SO, WHAT NEXT?

There are lots of things to do in the rain but of the very many things to do, visiting Eden must not be one of them. Really. Spare yourself. Eden is lovely. Less so when it is rammed full of fed up, wet, steaming holidaymakers and children voicing their opinions at the top of their lungs. Really, you may as well be camping. Similarly, people seem to flock to large supermarkets, Cornish Market World and Trago. Again, do not do this to yourself. It's very hard to understand why people come on holiday to stand with their entire family looking at the shelves in Asda in wonderment. But then I don't understand camping either.

Oh, and try to avoid going very far in your car. Everyone gets in their car and the roads grind to an absolute halt. Don't believe me? Try it.

So, what type of rain is it? Wet and still or wet and windy.[4]

WET AND STILL IS EXCELLENT. WELL, IT'S NOT BUT WE CAN WORK WITH IT.

You are going to get wet so go and get wetter. Go to the beach and learn to surf. Go to a harbour and book yourself onto a sea life safari boat trip. Head to one of the large rivers and hire a kayak and explore the estuaries. Go swimming. Bude and Penzance have two of the very finest outdoor swimming pools in the country.

Explore a part of Cornwall you have never heard of. Head up onto the moors if it's overcast, there are lots of great walks up there with some really fabulous pubs as well. Have a look at Walks 6 & 7. Mooch about a village, leave your car at the outskirt's car park.[5]

Go and find a field and slide around in the grass, go find some puddles and splash around. Find a cycle path and see who can make the biggest bow wave. You are going to get wet so why not remember how much fun it was when you were eight. Being cold and wet is only fun for a while. If you are out for the day, pack a change of clothes and stop somewhere for hot food.

WET AND WINDY. AH, THE DRAMATIC OPTION.

A fine choice but it does hamper your options a bit. Grab a camera, find somewhere safe and go watch the waves crashing in. Can't stress the "safe" bit enough. A harbour wall is NOT safe nor is anywhere near the actual waves. [6]

Wet and windy doesn't tend to last all day which means you can at least stay dry. If the weather is really beastly then just hunker down. Pull out a jigsaw puzzle, play snap for shots, read a book, put on a box set, make soup.

INSIDERS TIPS

Cornwall is a peninsula; the weather often splits along the spine that runs down the centre of Cornwall. Many times, if it is gloomy on the south coast then it's sunny on the north coast and vice versa.

The rain never lasts everywhere. Sitting indoors waiting for it to pass won't work. Just head out when you are ready and make the most of whatever the day turns out to be.

Have fun and welcome ☺

1. No, it doesn't. It means Welcome to Cornwall.
2. I once went on a touring camping holiday with my boyfriend in Scotland. It didn't rain but the cold at night was abysmal and I wasn't able to sleep properly. By day five we set up in the field of a B&B. After a massive row, where it was explained to me that I was wasting money and failing to understand the fun of camping, I headed off to the B&B and asked if I could book a bedroom. I slept and after sleeping I woke up warm, happy and single. The drive home was excruciating. [7]
3. It is not a fact.
4. There are so many more definitions of rain, but we'll just stick to these two large groups.
5. Outskirts. Yes right, outskirts summon up images of park and rides and depressing rows of charity shops and fried chicken takeaways. Our outskirts are normally a field with a portacabin manned by a bored teenager.
6. Please don't be that tragic statistic.
7. I have camped since. It has always been memorable. In the same way that dysentery is memorable.

SEASONAL RECIPES

There's nothing nicer than foraging for your own supper. Here are some of my favourite, and easiest recipes, from the most obvious and abundant foods you can find whilst out walking. These recipes are all rough and ready, food should be more freestyle.

SPRING – *Nettles*

Nettles are the bane of a walker's life but in early spring they are a tasty treat packed full of iron. Generally, people make a wonderfully vivid soup out of them, but I was passed this recipe from an old lady who I used to meet whilst walking our dogs. She swore that the new nettle shoots gave her strength for the year ahead.

RECIPE: *Stuffed Chicken Thighs*

Chop up an onion and bits of bacon and fry them in butter. Now, open up a boneless chicken thigh. Pack it with the mixture and a small handful of very young nettle shoots, removing any tough stalks. Don't worry about being stung, that goes when the nettles are cooked. Sprinkle over some oats, dried marjoram, salt and pepper, and a small knob of butter. Roll the thigh back up and tie up with string, to stop the contents falling out. Sprinkle some salt on the skin and then roast for around 40 minutes. Delicious.

SUMMER – *Elderflower*

Once you find a good elderflower patch, mark it well and come back to it again in autumn for the berries. In the spring the large white flouncy flower caps can be picked and turned into a delicious drink, either as a cordial or as champagne. Make sure you don't remove all the flower heads. Not everyone recognises elderflower. Just remember it's a bush or a tree. Large white flower heads growing up from the floor on a single stem are usually cow parsley.

RECIPE: *Elderflower champagne*

This is great fun and incredibly simple to make. There is a chance that the bottles may explode so use plastic bottles and store them somewhere, where they won't cause a problem. I follow the BBC recipe. Take a nice clean bucket, fill it with 4 litres of hot water and stir in 700g of sugar. When the sugar has dissolved, add the juice and zest of four lemons and two tablespoons of white wine vinegar. Then add 15 elderflower heads in full bloom, stir, cover with a towel and put aside for a day or two. Check if the mixture is becoming frothy, if it's not, add a pinch of dried yeast. Set aside for a few more days then strain and bottle in sterilised bottles. The Groslch ones are good or the 2lt fizzy drink bottles. Fill the bottles up leaving a good inch at the top, seal and store in a cool dry place. Drinkable after a week. If using plastic bottles keep an eye on how "tight" the bottle is becoming and release the cap a millimetre to reduce the pressure.

Even if you don't get the elderflower to ferment you will still have a lovely elder-flower drink.

AUTUMN – *Mushrooms*

First rule, if you aren't 100% certain of the identity, don't eat it. Wild mushrooms are an incredible treat and worth getting into. The easiest of all mushrooms to identify are Giant Puffballs. Quite simply they are large, white solid balls, about the size of a football, sometimes much larger. Usually growing in grass in early autumn. Nothing else looks remotely similar. Another very tasty mushroom that has no nasty lookalikes is the Cauliflower Fungus, found in conifer forests at the base of trees. Tricky to clean and best eaten young, not yellow and decaying.

RECIPE: *Simple mushrooms*

Slice, then fry in salt, butter and maybe a bit of garlic. Nothing more complicated than that. I love going on a morning walk and coming home with breakfast.

WINTER – *Mussels*

Mussels can be eaten at most times of the year but it's lovely to have such a tasty harvest in the bleakest months. Mussels should be avoided if there isn't an R in the month which is just another way to say avoid picking in the hotter months when the shells could form bacteria in the sun. Pick at low tide, go right down to the water's edge, this is where the largest mussels are, and don't pick anything shorter than an inch. If you pick at low tide at the furthest edge, then your harvest will have spent most of its time under water, rather than exposed to the sun. Pick and choose, do not clear out a patch. When you get home, empty them into a large container of water, discard any that open. Clean your mussels by yanking out the beard. This is the piece of seaweed that the mussel anchored itself to the rocks with. You may have removed these when you picked them, either way, you don't want to cook or eat them.

RECIPE: *Mussels PDQ*

Clean the mussels, removing the beard and put them in water. Put to one side until ready to cook. Now finely chop a bunch of shallots (or onions or leeks) and fry them gently in butter. Add the mussels and pour over wine or cider, and cover with a tight lid. You need enough liquid to give a depth of around one centimetre. You are not trying to boil them, you are steaming them. After five to ten minutes, serve! Bin any mussels that didn't open. Pour the cooking liquid over the mussels and maybe serve with chopped parsley and crusty bread. Proper fast food.

RECOMMENDED READING

Reading a story set in the place where you are staying / living, always adds an extra something. When the author describes a scene, you are instantly drawn into the book, especially when you can actually see it, not just imagine it! The following great stories are all set in this area and make for a great read.

Jamaica Inn – Daphne du Maurier

The House on the Strand – Daphne du Maurier

Castle Dor – Arthur Quiller-Couch & Daphne du Maurier

The Wind in the Willows – Kenneth Graham

Falling Creatures – Katherine Stansfield

Green Smoke – Rosemary Manning

Blue – Lisa Glass

OS Map 106

OS Map 107

OS Map 108

OS Map 109

OS Map 111

MORE BY LIZ HURLEY

CORNISH WALKS SERIES:

WALKING IN THE MEVAGISSEY AREA
9780993218033 | https://amzn.to/2FsEVXN

WALKING IN THE FOWEY AREA
9780993218040 | https://amzn.to/2r6bDtL

WALKING WITH DOGS BETWEEN TRURO AND FOWEY
9780993218057 | https://amzn.to/2jd83tm

TOP WALKS IN MID CORNWALL
9780993218064 | https://amzn.to/2LTxUI8

TOP WALKS IN EAST CORNWALL
9780993218088 | https://amzn.to/2XeBNZf

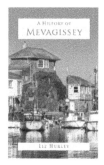

A HISTORY OF MEVAGISSEY
An engaging and informative history of Mevagissey.

For over eight hundred years, Mevagissey has flourished beside the south Cornish coastline. It was, in its heyday, a globally significant port, lighting the streets of London in the eighteenth century and feeding the homes of Europe. It has been battered by freak storms and a cholera outbreak but has continued, unbroken, contributing in no small part to the colonisation of the world by Cornish men and women.

This potted history gives an insight into the history of the village and takes a humorous look behind the scenes, revealing what it is like to actually live and work in Cornwall's second largest fishing port. It debunks a few myths and introduces some lively, tall tales, as told through local voices.

Available in bookshops.
Paperback: 978-0993218026 | Digital: https://amzn.to/2r5VlkA

SCRIBBLES FROM THE EDGE
When everyday life is anything but every day.

Liz Hurley gathers together her newspaper columns to deliver a collection of fast, funny reads. Join in as you share the highs and lows of a bookseller, dog lover and mother in Britain's finest county. This treasure trove of little gems moves from lifestyle pieces on living day-to-day behind the scenes in the UK's number one tourist destination, to opinion pieces on education, current affairs, science, politics and even religion. Watching the sun set over a glowing beach isn't quite so much fun when you are trying to find the keys your child hid in the sand, and the tide is coming in!

Join in and discover just how hard it is to surf and look glamorous at the same time. Batten down the hatches as she lets off steam about exploding cars and rude visitors. Laugh along and agree or disagree with Liz's opinion pieces, as you discover that although life might not be greener on the other side, it's a lot of fun finding out.

Available in bookshops.
Paperback: 978-0993218002 | Digital: https://amzn.to/2ji2UQZ

LOSING IT IN CORNWALL

The second collection of columns from Liz Hurley, still scribbling away on the edge. Still trying to hold it together. From serious to silly her columns cover all that life throws at us. A perfect selection of little titbits, to pick up and put down or read straight through.

Available in bookshops.
Paperback: 978-0993218019 | Digital: https://amzn.to/2r4eHGG

HELLO AND THANK YOU

Getting to know my readers is really rewarding, I get to know more about you and enjoy your feedback; it only seems fair that you get something in return, so if you sign up for my newsletter you will get various free downloads, depending on what I am currently working on, plus advance notice of new releases. I don't send out many newsletters, and I will never share your details. If this sounds good, click on the following: www.lizhurleywrites.com

I'm also on all the regular social media platforms so look me up.
#lizhurleywrites
#dreamingofcornwall

GET INVOLVED!

Join Walkers Talk Back on Facebook, to read about the next book in the walking series. Suggest routes, give feedback, receive advance copies. Better yet, share photos and feedback of the walks you enjoyed.
https://www.facebook.com/groups/841952742623247/

Did you enjoy this book? You can make a big difference.

Reviews are very powerful and can help me build my audience. Independent authors have a much closer relationship with their readers, and we survive and thrive with your help.

If you've enjoyed this book, then please let others know.

If you read it online leave a review on the site where you purchased it.

Thanks for helping,
Liz